Pure Unlimited Love

Pure Unlimited Love

Science and the Seven Paths to Inner Peace

By Stephen G. Post

Foreword by
HIS HOLINESS THE DALAI LAMA

Copyright © 2025 Stephen G. Post

All rights reserved. No part of this book may be reproduced, stored in a retrieval system, or transmitted in any form or by any means, electronic or mechanical, including photocopying, recording, or otherwise, without the written permission of the publisher.

Unless otherwise noted, the Scripture quotations are from New Revised Standard Version Bible, copyright © 1989 National Council of the Churches of Christ in the United States of America. Used by permission. All rights reserved worldwide.

Scripture quotations marked KJV are taken from the King James Version, public domain.

Certain names have been changed, as have potentially identifying characteristics.

Some dialogue has been recreated.

Morehouse Publishing
19 East 34th Street
New York, NY 10016
www.churchpublishing.org

Morehouse Publishing is an imprint of Church Publishing Incorporated.

Cover design by David Baldeosingh Rotstein
Typeset by Westchester Publishing Services

ISBN 978-1-64065-830-1 (hardcover)
ISBN 978-1-64065-832-5 (eBook)

Library of Congress Control Number: 2025938241

Contents

Foreword vii
Introduction ix

1 The First Path: May You Give and Glow 1
2 The Second Path: May You Heal with Kindness 35
3 The Third Path: May You Follow Your Callings 63
4 The Fourth Path: May You Raise Kind Children 95
5 The Fifth Path: May You Know the One Mind 127
6 The Sixth Path: May You Cherish the Gift of Nature . . . 157
7 The Seventh Path: May You Honor the Spirit
   of Freedom 185

Epilogue 211
Acknowledgments 215
About the Author 217
About the Institute for Research on Unlimited Love 221
Notes 223

Foreword

THE DALAI LAMA

An excessive focus on materialism and neglect of spiritual values such as love, compassion, and generosity have, I believe, prevented us from realizing our potential as a human society. While technological and scientific advancements have contributed to a better quality of life for many, the lack of attention to our inner lives is reflected in the persistent and pervasive emotional troubles and the growing socioeconomic and ideological divides at the root of so many of the problems affecting us today.

Various spiritual traditions and thinkers have, for millennia, understood how the nature and function of consciousness, and an appreciation of the interdependent nature of our world, are fundamental to human flourishing. However, it is only in recent decades that modern science has begun to address these topics. It has been my privilege to explore these ideas with leading physicists, neuroscientists, and other thinkers. It has been very encouraging to me to see the real possibility for a convergence of science and spirituality to benefit humanity.

As there is still much work to be done in this area, I'm pleased to see that noted author Dr. Stephen G. Post is addressing themes such as consciousness and interconnectedness in his new book about Seven Paths to Inner Peace through serving others, healing with kindness, following callings, raising kind children, knowing the inner mind, cherishing the gift of nature, and honoring the spirit of freedom through the Golden Rule. It is my hope that this book will contribute to the flourishing of humanity.

His Holiness the Dalai Lama

Introduction

Every morning around dawn, I rise to meditate prayerfully for about an hour. I begin by breathing slowly and deeply while relaxing and move on to envisioning the people I will encounter over the course of the day with an emphasis on the particular expression of love they might most benefit from based on what I know they have been experiencing of late. For instance, would a colleague appreciate more acknowledgment for always making time to help others with their teaching and research? Does a friend need someone to quietly listen to their painful concerns about a beloved teenage son who is relapsing into drug abuse? I imagine likely conversations with the nearest and dearest, like family members. And I ask myself, *How do I need to manifest love on this day?*

Picking the right form of love for the people in my life is important because love in its many forms heals individuals and communities. We seldom hear people in most contexts of everyday life speaking directly about love in its highest meaning, but we always hear conversations about the ten common forms it takes, such as celebrating meaningful accomplishments, providing compassionate care, forgiveness for those burdened by their inevitable mistakes, attentive listening, "carefrontation" for those who need a love that nudges them to stick with their core values, general helpfulness, loyalty especially for people who have been betrayed, respect, tasteful mirthfulness that can help someone reframe their perspective on events, and creativity especially for those who are struggling with their projects. This list of ten forms of love is not meant to be complete, but it shows that love heals in all of its variety of concrete expressions.

Times of Crisis

These are times of social change and crisis, and they are stressful. Such times come and go in every era and are not usually all negative because they allow new expressions of love to burst forth from the mud. The Buddhists have a saying that without mud there can be no lotus blossoming, with the lotus being a symbol of purity, resilience, and creative love. But before the new day arrives, many feel disoriented, confused, and stressed. We may feel that "the centre cannot hold" and that aspects of our common culture are about to "fall apart," as the poet William Butler Yeats put it.[1] In this age of anxiety, people become confused about what constitutes a good and flourishing life. An overwhelming uncertainty sweeps away values and behaviors that were once held onto as matters of common faith, such as the American dream. In the chaos, truth departs, and the half-truths arrive to fill an emotional void. People generally feel more secure when their beliefs and values at least *seem* to be certain, even if presented as more concrete than they really are. When things fall apart, people experience separation anxieties as previous attachments fade. But it is also true that the sun always rises. There are crises in this world, many of which we cannot alleviate, but we can always do much to alleviate the crises in our minds.

In our hyperpolarized culture and society, many of us have stopped listening to one another, grown short-tempered, and lost the redemptive sense of community that makes a place for love despite our differences in opinion and politics. But with more will and effort we can resuscitate humility and love in the home, the workplace, the community, schools, the environment, the government, and within our own hearts, where it really must begin. How can we find and maintain an inner peace, even in times of overwhelming anxiety? The answer begins with love—and not just any love, mind you, but with Pure Unlimited Love. This is the time for love to rise more beautifully than ever before. I do not believe in some poorly defined "new age," but I do believe that the lotuses are blooming anew and pointing to an age of Pure Unlimited Love.

What Is Pure Unlimited Love?

Pure Unlimited Love is not the love we have for chocolate or designer sneakers but an energy so divine and powerful it can move mountains. In our daily lives we experience it in often simple yet profound forms. *Pure love in its undifferentiated essence is this: When the security and well-being of another is as real or meaningful to us as our own, and sometimes even more so, we are within the field of love.*

We can all hopefully relate to this definition, whether it involves love of self, friendship, family life, parenthood, a special calling to assist a needy group, or affirming our shared humanity. I am a believer in love of self, but not when it takes up all the space in the room and crowds other people out. We can also extend love of this sort to other species and to nature. How we treat our pets and nature more generally matters, and any cruelty to nonhuman animals probably spills over into human interactions. I believe that we thrive best in love for the Supreme Being, ourselves, our neighbors, and nature. These are the four loves that lead to fulfillment.

Pure Unlimited Love is "pure" of heart, being untainted by manipulation, exploitation, or any intent other than flourishing. It is extensive and all-inclusive of our shared humanity, although it does not ignore the nearest and dearest who require our special affection and responsibility. Yet it leans outward, never myopic. It is wise and effective. It is enduring, rather than unstable or turning on and off like a flickering bulb. It does not fade away, and in these ways must have its Source in something more reliable than human nature disconnected from the divine. In a metaphysical sense, it is said to underlie all of reality, or so say the mystics and considerable numbers of physicists and mathematicians. Often, Pure Unlimited Love does not feel like it originates in our own selves so much as from some surprising inbreaking power invading our inner being or consciousness as we consent to it. Pure Unlimited Love breaks through to us as a spiritual energy that sends the message that we are more cherished in this journey of life than we sometimes think.

I asked my very insightful physician friend, Jeffrey S. Trilling, MD, with whom I teach a course on compassionate care in the medical school, to describe Pure Unlimited Love. He answered after a few minutes pause, stating that such love is not just human emotion, but rather is "what you see when you close your eyes in this world for the last time, hopefully."[2] It is the light that about a third of adults tell us about after they have been resuscitated following a prolonged loss of consciousness due to cardiac arrest.[3] For those who self-report the experience, this "light" surrounds them with the warmth of a love that is something much more than human love, with all its limitations and reversals. And it is something that the mystics report they experience in the inner peace of prayer and meditation, a love that feels like it is flowing through them rather than coming from them, and that energizes them to alleviate suffering when it takes the form of the most intense and tireless compassion. They tell us that to feel Pure Unlimited Love is to feel the divine itself, and that "God is love."[4]

Not everyone can be expected to believe this, but they can experiment with it in meditational states—with eyes closed or open and by focusing on the center of the forehead just above the eyes, allowing the ocean of silence to bring them into a quiet peace where awareness of the body recedes. Known by psychiatrists as the oceanic state, such quietism is described widely across the centuries. Spiritual people view it as connecting our individual consciousness with the One Mind, also known as "god." The psychiatrist may think of this experience as illusion, but they can never deny that it is widespread across cultures, and that ubiquity should tell us something.

Pure Unlimited Love is literally the life-giving force that leads to meaning, annuls loneliness by making solitude a blessing, and is the best antidote to the destructive emotions and tendencies that plague people today as they often have from the beginning of human history. Love is goodness itself, the loftiest form of liberation and freedom from the cynical and hurtful elements of our culture, and it is the strongest alternative to hopelessness, resentment, hate, insanity, bitterness, and the crazy dance of violence that persists between individuals and groups. In short, we simply cannot flourish in the absence of Pure Unlimited Love, although it is not something that we always notice as underlying its various forms of expression. It is the one thing that gives depth to all the good that we do, and makes them fulfilling for us and for the world.

Experiencing Pure Unlimited Love: Into the Mystic

Pure Unlimited Love is all around us and very much within us, but to realize this we have to develop spiritual practices and daily lifestyles that allow us to notice it in the present, freed from the pressures of time and relentless human doing that blind us to the dignity of simply being present, or of the validity of simply being. We can access this energy despite the countervailing forces in even the most negative of cultures. We human beings radiate in connection with Pure Unlimited Love, which occurs when we stay focused on the Oneness within and honor the spark of the divine that is the essence of every human consciousness and mind. When we center ourselves on an inner spiritual practice, we can generate pure love and exude dignity. Through such practices we open the doors of our mind and heart to be invaded by the light and warmth of a pure love that feels quite different and well beyond the normal repertoire of human creatures.

Although Pure Unlimited Love is available to all of us, most people experience it only fleetingly. Still, even in our secular world, our highly discussed national survey of American adults, conducted by Matthew T. Lee, Margaret Poloma, and myself, showed that about 80 percent claim to have experienced such divine love directly or otherwise through others at least once, and about 40 percent claim to have experienced it more than once. Twenty percent of people experience this daily, and about 10 percent report that they feel this all the time.[5] But this Pure Unlimited Love experience, while it can be completely sporadic, can also be primed with spiritual practices, such as mindfulness, meditation, prayer, and just noticing its presence in the heart. So I've offered a framework we can all use to nurture this gift and find inner peace from it regardless of what's going on around us. Like the lotus, we can each bloom above the murkiness of the world in hope, purity, and inner beauty. The framework consists of seven paths upon which we can manifest Pure Unlimited Love in its ten primary forms. These Seven Paths and Ten Forms begin for me with a morning meditation, one we can use to focus our inner compass before we get caught up in the stressors and tensions of the typical day.

The Seven Paths are presented in the form of a meditational mantra:

The Seven Paths

1. May You Give and Glow.
2. May You Heal with Kindness.
3. May You Follow Your Callings.
4. May You Raise Kind Children.
5. May You Know the One Mind.
6. May You Cherish the Gift of Nature.
7. May You Honor the Spirit of Freedom.

Following these paths opens our hearts and minds to the Pure Unlimited Love that spiritual people call the divine. I do envision people in meditation and ask myself if they seem to be walking these paths, and if so, are they walking them well.

Ten Forms or Manifestations of Pure Unlimited Love in the Image of a Wheel

Pure Unlimited Love is an energy, the ultimate energy, and it goes by many names: Original Mind, Ultimate Reality, Infinite Mind, Source, One Mind, Higher Being, Higher Power, Creator, Universal Spirit, Ground of Being, "God," Agape Love, Divine Mind, Sacred Heart, the Supreme Being. It really does not matter too much what you call this sacred energy. The Hebrew Bible says, "I am who I am," and it is written that "God is love," which is the fullest description and one that should suffice.[6]

The ten forms of love are so much easier to talk about than "love" itself because the forms transpose the language of love into everyday experiences of celebration, compassionate care, forgiveness, attentive listening, "carefrontation," helpfulness, loyalty, respect, mirth, and creativity. In music the same melody can be "transposed" into various different keys. It remains constant but is also distinctive in each key.

When we practice spiritual techniques that invite a deeper connection with the One Mind underlying and permeating this universe, and also in special way with our deepest being or soul, we become more "in tune" with this Pure Unlimited Love. Then we do not have to work so hard at making this connection because Pure Unlimited Love is able to more or less invade our consciousness, and all we have to do is consent to this energy and allow it to flow more easily.

To illustrate the different forms of Pure Unlimited Love, I created the Wheel of Love. This tool has been useful for the many people who have no clear idea what we might mean by Pure Unlimited Love, but they understand all its forms more readily: I do not go to work using the words "Pure Unlimited Love," but I do speak of all the forms of love as a style of appreciative leadership and team building.

I keep this wheel image with ten spokes on the wall of my home office and in front of me during those early morning meditations as I contemplate those I am likely to encounter that day—including any adversaries. And I love my adversaries because I know they are in my life for a reason—to bring out my best.

My family also uses the wheel when we need reflection. The effect is to create positive solutions, avoid meltdowns, and remain

scream free. What might family culture look like if everyone had a Wheel of Love magnet on their refrigerator door around which they could gather and talk things through? Or how about we post the Wheel of Love in every classroom as a cultural centerpiece?

A Spiritual Dress Rehearsal for the Day

My morning meditation is a spiritual dress rehearsal for the day, and it sets the tone in an essential way. I can still get a little off course under pressure—perhaps not always being as loving as I had intended—but living a life of reasonable consistent loving-kindness and dignity becomes a lot easier through this internal discipline. Intentionally trying to show love and kindness using the Ten Forms on the Wheel makes me far more mindful of my interactions than I would be had I rushed to the office without having paused to give my day and my encounters a second thought.

In the evening if time permits I might quietly ask myself a question for each of the Seven Paths:

> Did I feel uplifted in giving with kindness?
> Did I speak with the tone and heart of a healer?
> Did I stay focused on my callings or get pulled off course?
> Did I set an example of kindness for younger people who showed up my door?
> Did I maintain awareness of the One Mind and not get swept away by the world?
> Did I feel a sense of awe as I encountered nature and the skies?
> Did I honor and fulfill the duties and responsibilities of freedom?

And as time permits, I will ask myself questions about my living up to the spokes on the Wheel:

> Did I take those few minutes to join in the celebration down the hall, or did I drive to a student's wedding?
> Did I ask someone if I was right in thinking that they might be suffering, and if so how?
> Did I let go of bitterness and forgive someone who seemed to be apologetic or even not so apologetic?
> Did I listen well instead of interrupting someone?

Did I diplomatically "carefront" an old friend who was not living up to their values?
Did I lend someone a helping hand in some simple encounter?
Did I tell someone that loyalty really matters and that they can count on me?
Did I respect someone by looking and listening to them more carefully?
Did I thoughtfully and in good taste share a little joke today?
Did I affirm someone's creative accomplishments today?

No one has been or ever will be perfect in the forms of love. I am not a believer in human perfection, but when we make the right kind of spiritual connection with "god" we can do a lot better. Being mindful about the forms of love and even journaling about them achieves several goals: These forms prime us to use the best form of love for the right people at the right time. They keep us focused on not only who but what needs loving-kindness—perhaps a pet, a garden, or a calling. They keep us on a personal path to inner peace. And they help us cultivate love in every aspect of our world and to be sorry when we don't.

By practicing these meditations, we stay centered and carry an inner peace regardless of what's going on around us. This state of being is essential during a time when people are suffering, and even dying, from anxiety disorders, nature deficit disorder, and a doomsday mentality. Despite politics, social division, climate change, nuclear weapons, deadly viruses, the dangers of artificial intelligence, and the looming threat that this is the end of times, we can do our small part to make the world a better place, one intentional loving act at a time with a spirituality that opens our hearts to, as the Hindus like to say, "the Supreme," or as the Native Americans like to put it, "the Great Spirit."

The Wheel Rolling on Seven Paths

These Seven Paths are not random. They seem to be the essential ones in most well-lived lives, although not everyone follows these paths to the same degree. On each path the goal is to apply the most pertinent forms of love.

It's possible to tell when someone is practicing love along the Seven Paths, whether they are aware of it or not. People who feel Pure Unlimited Love tend to carry themselves with a graceful poise; they are often described as "looking dignified." They hold themselves with dignity and are too active being kind to engage in corrupt, harmful, or humiliating behaviors or speech that de-dignifies others and themselves as well. This dignity includes virtues such as integrity, respect, and honesty. People of pure love have a powerful spiritual and moral sense of equal regard for all people. In this Oneness, they find serenity and purpose. This form of dignity is present whenever kindly love radiates in our lives. These are people who are living in active connection with the divine. As our national survey of adult Americans showed conclusively, those who self-report an experience of the divine also report a quickening of active compassion and purpose.

By mindfully cultivating Pure Unlimited Love along these paths, we can know dignity, for the paths break down the walls between self and deeper self, between self and others, and between self and nature. It is not that we always arrive at the end of a path, but rather that as we walk the paths, we care for our fellow travelers, forming communities of virtue along the way.

Mindful meditation or prayer is a good way to begin living out love on these Seven Paths. Attending group worship is another good way to begin. Fulfillment begins in the mind and heart, which are like temples that we can beautify with color and light, creating images of loving kindness and living more fully. There are many ancient passages to support this process of thinking with the whole self. One of the best known is: "As a person thinketh in their heart, so they are."[7]

I have done research since 1982 on the theme of this higher experience of love, including a dissertation at the University of Chicago. This interest really goes back to my years in high school in New Hampshire, where I wrote my "sixth form" senior paper on love in St. Augustine. The other side of me was focused on biology. For many years I have enjoyed the environment of several major national academic medical centers as a professor of medical humanities and compassionate care at the interface of science and religious practices, founded and directed new programs, served as president and cofounder of a major research nonprofit, served as a board member of several foundations, including the John Templeton Foundation, and traveled the United States and the world to help preserve dignity for deeply forgetful people (those with dementia). Since the 1980s, I've done my imperfect best as a husband and a father. I have followed my callings fairly rigorously and found some enjoyable success.

When the ten forms or expressions of loving heart and one mindedness are combined with the Seven Paths, we have all we need to create a cultural movement centered on the spiritual ideal of Pure Unlimited Love—saving lives, improving mental health, and opening ourselves and others to inner peace as best we can. I am not utopian, but like most people, I would like us to do better.

CHAPTER 1

The First Path: May You Give and Glow

> "Scent lingers on the hands of those who deliver flowers."
>
> —Ancient Chinese proverb

> "I'm convinced of this: Good done anywhere is good done everywhere."
>
> —Maya Angelou

Some years ago, I delivered a speech in a Manhattan hotel to a group of bereaved widows and widowers. The subject was how helping others allows the helpers to overcome grief more quickly than nonhelpers. I told a few stories about kind giving and described some of the research that confirms these findings. It went well, but at the conclusion, a widower in the back of the packed ballroom stood up and yelled, "I don't care what you say, buddy. I don't do nuthin' for nuthin'!" I thought to myself that I really was not in Cleveland anymore.

This critic required a diplomatic and compassionate response: "Does life for you boil down entirely to the art of the deal?"

I asked. With the other attendees all ears, he acknowledged that he approached every interaction with this transactional mindset but added that he had never been a very happy person. I suggested that he might try replacing this "I don't do nuthin' for nuthin'" at least in his personal life with an opposite sentiment: "I give and glow." Inwardly, givers are better off emotionally and physically, whether people return the kindness or not. Although you can never count on reciprocation, you can always count on the meaning and the inner glow of giving, and that can more than suffice.

"Glowing" is my synonym for well-being and inner peace. Maybe the word "radiance" captures it just as well. As the visionary philanthropist John Templeton once said, "Who are the happiest people you have ever met? Let us write down the names of ten persons who continually bubble over with happiness, and we will probably find that most are men and women who radiate love for everyone."[8]

A lot of things can make us glow—a baby's smile, a majestic mountain, being fully present with a loved one. But very often, *glowing is a paradoxical or unintended byproduct of giving with kindness.* The proven truth is that we can glow anywhere if we are helping others. This is the one source of resilience in our lives that we can most depend on and that is always available for the choosing. I know because giving and glowing is the general subject of more than fifty scientific papers I've had published in medical and psychology journals over the past four decades. It is also how I survive life's biggest challenges.

Holocaust survivor and author Victor Frankl is a well-known example of giving and glowing even in the most difficult of times. When I was in college, I heard him deliver a speech about how even when he was in a German prison camp with his fellow Jews, he found meaning, hope, and resilience in sharing his very meager bit of food with other prisoners who looked even more emaciated than he was. His book *Man's Search for Meaning* remains an inspiring classic to this day.

Kind giving is a great way to expand the canvas of our lives in difficult moments, turning negatives into positives, heartaches into peace. Kind giving is the best way to overcome challenges big and small. When we give kindly, we are freed from preoccupation with life's unavoidable disappointments and adversities. The volume of our generosity in time or dollars does not matter. Small helping acts are as beneficial to the giver as big ones because it is not how much we give that creates inner peace but how much kindness we pour into it. Kindness is close to love, but not quite as deep, although the two are closely related. If we're just going through the motions of giving without much heart, or because it is required of us, giving can be burdensome. "Loving-kindness," or *chesed*, is a big part of Jewish ethics, and this combination is found in various other traditions because for many people to speak of kindness is to speak of love in its essence.

So, what does loving-kind giving look like?

Giving from the Heart

Kind giving is much more than an external action, and the kindness makes all the difference. It includes "gentle curiosity"—an expression created by my colleague Dr. Trilling—about the well-being and life narrative of the recipient. This is a curiosity that encompasses a readiness to listen and make their lives in some small way a little better by virtue of the encounter. A good goal is to move through each day with this loving-kindness in place.

Kind people in our highly intercultural and complex society are typically humble personally, intellectually, and culturally. They are eager to learn and serve, and they listen attentively. The ones who think of themselves as always right tend to leave little space in the room for others. Arrogant and divisive, they interrupt others as soon as they start expressing themselves. Humility does not at all mean humiliation, but it does mean thinking of yourself less. Thinking of self too much can be plain boring. These humility tips double as kindness tips:

Admit mistakes.
Embrace differences.
Appreciate others.
Take advice.
Listen a lot before you talk.
Don't interrupt.
Ask respectful questions rather than offer too-easy answers.
Respond, don't react.

As boys, my friends and I used to go snapper fishing on the Great South Bay off Long Island. Occasionally, someone would catch a blowfish, also known as a pufferfish. Once it sensed danger, it would blow up like a big balloon in a millisecond. I was amazed at how much hard work it took for that blowfish to self-inflate. It reminded me of a neighbor boy named Ray who was always so busy inventing stories about his exploits. He never seemed to stop making things up about his imaginary blown-up self. This took up most of his energy. He had no time to be kind, or to be peaceful or free of heart, and he was always interrupting us.

One day I said to him, "Hey, Ray, you talk too much, and it worries me." This may sound harsh, but at the time we were all singing a hit song by Joe Jones entitled "You Talk Too Much," and it was playing on the radio daily. "Listen to others a little more, Ray, and count to seven before saying anything. Try it for a while and see how you feel." The other guys all agreed. Ray gave it a try and found that he was making—and keeping—more friends. He became a more successful and purposeful student and a much more respected member of our peaceful Peninsula Drive gang. Ray started to Give and Glow. When Ray died in his seventies, about four hundred people attended his funeral. I heard that many who spoke there described Ray as radiant. No one thought of him as a blowfish. My little "carefrontation" intervention early on in his life seemed to work well for him over the years.

Human beings can act like blowfish, but we are also a bit like those hardwired glow sticks you find at a fair or circus—those thick, translucent plastic tubes containing substances that light up when you bend the stick. This inner quality is what makes glow sticks glow. Likewise, kind giving produces a chemical reaction within the brain, activating the brain's mesolimbic pathway and turning off the pathways of destructive negative emotions. People who are actively helping in a state of loving-kindness are feeling inner peace and can resist the pitfall of destructive emotions. Kind giving has the unique ability to defy the second law of thermodynamics, which states that as energy is transferred, it is wasted.

The most noticeable marker of kind giving is the increasing radiance it creates in the giver. People who give without kindness don't feel this radiance. They give but not with their whole selves. But there are studies of people who gave just because it was required of them, and soon the light of kindness turned on, and they discovered that "in the giving of self lies the paradoxical discovery of a deeper self."[9] Our research shows that there are many other benefits as well.

The Benefits of Kind Giving

I was once a brief consultant for the 2010 online survey of a national sample of 4,582 American adults, 18 years and older, sponsored by United Healthcare/VolunteerMatch Do Good Live Well.[10] The survey indicated that 41 percent of Americans volunteered in the year 2009 for an average of 100 hours per year; 69 percent of the participants reported donating money in addition to volunteering. The results of the survey are telling:[11]

- 73 percent said that volunteering "lowered my stress levels" (serenity). Many of us are completely caught up in the pressures of making ends meet, paying the bills, running from point A to point B, or just handling challenges. When we help others, we tend to forget about the self and the problems of the self. Helpers are free of self-centered chronological time. By focusing on the needs of others, they move into the *now* of helping.
- 89 percent agreed that "volunteering improved my sense of well-being."
- 92 percent felt an "enriched sense of purpose in life."
- 68 percent said volunteering "made me feel physically healthier." This is a robust finding. Many of these volunteers are doing work that requires ambulation or other forms of activity that frees them from a more sedentary culture.
- 77 percent said that volunteering "improves emotional health."
- 78 percent said that volunteering "helps recovery from loss and disappointment." A few weeks after the December 2012 shootings, I drove up to the Sandy Hook Elementary School in Newtown, Connecticut, to reflect on the scene. The people in Starbucks were still in tears. I noticed a bumper sticker on

a glass door and on some cars: "WE ARE SANDY HOOK. WE CHOSE LOVE." The people of Newtown found resilience and hope in compassionate love, even in the depths of loss and anguish. Medical evidence now confirms that helping others consistently predicts resilience, especially in hard times.

- 96 percent of participants felt happier. Because so many Americans struggle with unhappiness and depression, any activity that makes 96 percent of participants feel happier is worth taking seriously. The association between giving and happiness has become so widely accepted that the 2016 *World Happiness Report* includes generosity as one of six categories measured.[12]
- Volunteering: a majority of respondents reported improved sleep and deeper friendships; reduced anxiety and helplessness.
- 25 percent volunteer through their workplace, and 76 percent of them feel better about their employer as a result. Many companies can and do encourage employee volunteerism. Over the course of about six weeks, volunteerism is associated with positive relationships, better attitudes toward companies and employers, greater job satisfaction, strengthened work teams, greater competency and creativity, lower need for mental healthcare, easier employee recruitment, employee retention, and elevated interactions with customers, leading to a better bottom line.

If a pill promised this much benefit, investors would mark it a "strong buy," a natural vitamin for the soul. But no existing pill does this much good.

Kindness is something we can actively do—rather than something we passively swallow. Psychologists distinguish between "active hope" and "passive hope," the former being beneficial and the latter not so much. When we are active agents, generating our own hope, we're much better off than when hoping someone "out there" will come through for us

How might we interpret these survey findings?

Rx: The Two-Hour Shift Effect

All this research has given us a general dosage for volunteering: *100 hours per year, spread out to about two hours per week.* This is enough time to get fully immersed in an activity on a regular and sustainable basis. Individuals differ psychologically and physically, and they must balance their varying commitments. There is no particular dose of volunteering that should be prescribed for every individual other than to state, as I often have, "that a couple of hours per week seems to make an impact on well-being." I refer to this as the "two-hour shift effect," but this is a composite figure. Adolescents may just need one hour a week, while older adults in retirement may benefit most from three or four. Exceeding this threshold does not increase benefits.[13]

To emphasize, it is not the case that *the more one gives the better one feels.* One achieves the shift effect by performing a couple hours of helping actions that transform their mode of being and feeling. This illustrates a well-established (James-Lange) theory of emotional change through action, which states that emotions are caused by the brain's interpretations of bodily actions. This is why people suggest you smile even if you are not happy.

Simple acts of loving-kindness can transform us emotionally when we might otherwise get sucked down into despair and resentment. Emotions often follow actions, just as actions follow emotions. We have known this for more than a century. You do not have to go up to the highest mountain and meditate to find that inner glow. Modern psychologists have since 1992 demonstrated that if you perform kind acts, you are likely to experience the famous "helper's high," an emotional transition from negative states such as hostility and anger to positive states.[14]

The world becomes so much more interesting and engaging when we seek the happiness, security, and well-being of another. Selfishness and unkindness are just plain boring. But it is impossible to be bored if you love your neighbor and are busy helping them.

Kindness improves educational outcomes. We learn more when we tutor younger peers or are responsible for teaching in groups. I personally enjoyed tutoring young French-Canadian grade schoolers as a boy in New Hampshire—so much so that it motivated me to become an educator in my mid-teens. *Kindness can give us a great reason to develop our gifts,* such as when we give ourselves over to a special interest and perhaps make a positive difference in the world.

For example, in 1915, Dr. Edward Livingston Trudeau, grandfather of the great cartoonist Gary Trudeau, was dying of tuberculosis (TB). If this was going to kill him, he wanted to do his best to try and find a cure. His wife gave him her blessing to leave her and their two babies behind in New York City so he could go in solitude to the forests of the Adirondack Mountains. He was weak and feverish on the rugged trip to Au Sable Forks, where he was carried into his room at the Paul Smith's Hotel. He ate healthy food, spent a lot of time out on the porches in the fresh air, and found peace being surrounded by nature.

A year later, the young doctor returned to his family fifteen pounds heavier, with his TB no longer active. He moved his family to the North country, residing in a simple house on Lake Saranac, from which arose a community that created the first fresh-air sanitariums. It is now restored, as are the numerous "cure cottages" that surround it. He also built a laboratory to study *Mycobacterium tuberculosis*.

Kindness and the natural world, along with heathy diet, seemed to be the only successful treatment. Two renowned pulmonologists I encountered at Cleveland hospitals, including the world-famous Emanuel Wolinsky, MD, were cured during their medical school years in Lake Saranac and devoted themselves to finding new treatments throughout their careers. In healthcare we refer to individuals like Trudeau and Walinski as "wounded healers" because they draw on their experience with a particular illness to become outstanding and deeply compassionate healers. Of course, they are wise and never lead off speaking about their own illness experience, or even speak of it at all, but with wisdom they may speak of it at the right time when it can be helpful to the patient. It explains why they achieve so much for so many.

Kind giving reduces destructive and antisocial behaviors.[15] National population studies show that *we deepen friendships when we treat others with kindness.* Our friends are no longer the people we just hang out with; they are the ones with whom we find common cause and commitment. At last, we have serious friends, the kind who are loyal and want to keep us on our course and true to our higher selves. Surround yourself with these sorts of friends, and you can't help but be a big success in life.

Kindness to others is a source of hope. When we use our strengths to make a difference in the life of another, we have greater confidence in shaping the future. This is an active hope, rather than that passive variety that just waits around.

Kind giving creates dignity and worth. Our dignity is ours to claim when we treat another person with love. Human dignity lies chiefly in expanding the range and power of our greatest asset. We find significance in our lives in kind giving.

Studies of the brain indicate that when the circuits for kindness (the mesolimbic pathway) are turned on, *the circuits for bitterness and hostility turn off.* This gives meaning to the passage from 1 John 4:18, "Perfect love casts out fear." It casts out hatred, bitterness, hostility, vindictiveness, rage, and jealousy as well.

The best news is that *kind giving is not reserved for a few altruistic souls.* Everyone is called by nature to Give and Glow and hence take the path to fulfillment.[16]

Give and Glow is an inalienable and irreplaceable path of human fulfillment, inner freedom, and inner peace. This can be explained partly by our having evolved as a species in groups, where feelings of fulfillment would naturally evolve because helping behavior has a selective advantage in contributing to group functionality and success. Charles Darwin, in his 1871 book *The Descent of Man,* realized that our inclination to help and serve others with kindness and compassion was the result of evolutionary competition between groups. Human evolution, he recognized, is not just between individuals competing for some desired object. The more internal kindness and helping a group has within it, the better off it will be.[17]

Our biochemistry responds favorably to our actions of kind giving. Since 2000, robust research literature has demonstrated the health benefits of giving.[18] My original article on this subject has been cited by more than 1,500 other scientists and scholars and seems to have opened up this field of study. There are four brain chemicals associated with kind giving: (1) oxytocin (the hormone of trust and connectivity); (2) endorphins (neurotransmitters released by the pituitary gland and hypothalamus in the brain that as natural hormones alleviate pain, lower stress, improve mood, and elevate the sense of well-being); (3) serotonin (a neurotransmitter that regulates behaviors, mood, and memory); and (4) dopamine (a neurotransmitter released when people do something pleasurable or beneficial to others). This biochemistry of "care and connection" explains the findings in the United Healthcare survey cited above.[19]

But more than biology may be involved. For according to most spiritual traditions worldwide, when we help others, we are also helping ourselves, simply because we are all interwoven within the One Mind, or Consciousness. Kind giving goes with rather than against the grain of both group evolution and Consciousness itself. Ralph Waldo Emerson wrote, "No man [or woman] can sincerely help another without helping himself." Or as Oscar Wilde put it, echoing Plato, "To be good is to be in harmony with oneself." Thoreau wrote, "Goodness is the only investment that never fails." This wisdom is universal. It's good to be kind, and science says it's so.

A Quick Survey of Some Specific Populations

Kind giving is a vitamin pill for the soul that, while it can benefit anyone anywhere, is particularly healing for individuals with illnesses. For some years, I investigated "helper therapy," a concept coined by social psychologist Frank Reissman in 1965. Dr. Reissman defined the helper therapy principle after observing numerous self-help groups in which helping others is deemed essential to helping oneself—not only mentally, emotionally, and spiritually but physically. Alcoholics Anonymous (AA) is one such group.

Alcoholics Anonymous

The grassroots groups known as AA originated in the 1930s and today involve millions of people worldwide and have, over the years, expanded to include Narcotics Anonymous, Overeaters

Anonymous, and many more. AA is the oldest and largest self-help group in the United States. AA has been extremely successful, having saved countless people who might otherwise have died from their addiction. Members of AA follow the Twelve Steps, the last of which is to help others who are also struggling with addiction.

It is impossible to help someone else up a hill without walking up it yourself. This is the universal mindset of AA meetings, and has been posted on the meeting walls since the late 1930s. *Alcoholics Anonymous* (2nd Edition, 1955, p. 89), the core "big book," states that "practical experience shows that nothing will so much insure immunity from drinking as intensive work with other alcoholics." This practical use of helping others in recovery is at the center of a ten-year research project carried out with health psychologist Maria Pagano in the lead, which indicates that those in an AA meeting who are most engaged (high quartile) in service and helping have a 40 percent recovery rate after one year of involvement, whereas the low quartile helpers have about a 22 percent recovery rate. AA members have always known this, but the Pagano team was the first to prove it with science. The data were derived from a prospective study called Project MATCH, which examined different treatment options for alcoholics and evaluated their efficacy in preventing relapse. The authors found that "those who were helping were significantly less likely to relapse in the year following treatment."[20] Helping others doubles the likelihood of recovery from alcoholism in a one-year period.

Chronic Pain Sufferers

Individuals suffering from chronic pain experienced decreased pain intensity, levels of disability, and depression when they began to serve as peer volunteers for others suffering from chronic pain.[21] It is the case that helping others shifts a person's attention away from their pain. There is also a biochemistry involved that engages the endorphins, the body's natural painkillers, which are also associated with states of hope.[22]

Cardiology Patients

At the Duke Heart Center Patient Support Program, researchers concluded that former cardiac patients who make regular visits to help inpatient cardiac patients have a heightened sense of purpose and reduced levels of despair and depression, which are linked to mortality.[23] The Corporation for National & Community Service, which provides two million Americans of all ages and backgrounds with volunteer opportunities through Senior Corps, AmeriCorps, and Learn and Serve America, conducted a study using health and volunteer data from the US Census Bureau and the Centers for Disease Control and Prevention. Researchers found that "states with high volunteer rates also have lower rates of mortality and incidences of heart disease."[24]

Mental Health

Many state offices of mental health emphasize the role of helping others through involvement in self-help groups.[25] This kind of state initiative is reminiscent of the famous moral treatment era in the American asylums of the 1870s and '80s, when persons with melancholy and other ailments were treated with compassion and also, whenever possible, directly engaged in prosocial activities.[26] A great example of this today is Hopewell, a residential farm treatment center that I have been involved with at times. These residents help one another, stay close to nature on 350 acres, and practice small group dialogue centered on positive psychology, such as helping, kindness, forgiveness, gratitude, and wisdom.

Prescribing or recommending kind helping to patients is a valid contribution to preventive medicine and the basis of Social Prescribing—a movement to connect people with activities to improve health and well-being. The movement now exists in over thirty countries and is known to help combat loneliness, stress, and negative emotional states. It has been thoroughly described by Julia Hotz in her book, *The Connection Cure*.

Volunteering Across the Life Span

People of all ages—and across the life span—benefit from kind giving.

Young People

A significant investigation on happiness and health examined volunteering in adolescents. Just over one hundred tenth-grade students in an urban Vancouver high school were split into two equal size groups. One group volunteered regularly for ten weeks, and the other group was placed on a waiting list for volunteer opportunities. Researchers measured body mass index, inflammation, and cholesterol levels before and after the study. They also assessed mental health, mood, and empathy. The volunteers spent one hour per week helping school children in after-school programs (such as homework, cooking, cards, science, and sports clubs).

At the end of ten weeks, the students on the waitlist showed no change in their markers, but volunteering students had lower levels of inflammation, cholesterol, and body mass index. The volunteers who reported the greatest increases in empathy, altruistic behavior, and mental health saw the greatest reductions in the biological markers. When these markers are elevated, they are the first signs of cardiovascular disease, which is spreading in adolescents and limits their life expectancy. The results of this study support the premise that adolescents can benefit from a mere one hour of volunteering per week.[27]

I have substantiated this in dozens of studies over recent years. For example, when COVID-19 first hit in 2020, medical students were for the most part learning online and not interacting with patients. They found that volunteerism was an important mechanism to promote resilience, empathy, and general well-being in students. One student was sad that COVID kept her from seeing patients, and she organized her peers to do volunteer work engaging and entertaining patients online. This group published three major studies on how the answer to isolation and loneliness is volunteering in some way to help others.[28]

Teen opioid overdose is epidemic, and teen alcoholism and alcohol abuse are at extremely high levels. Evidence supporting the theory that the key to overcoming alcoholism in teens lies in service to others has been reported by the Pagano team mentioned earlier. I was honored to work with her team from Case, Harvard, and Stony Brook to produce more than forty peer-reviewed articles. Helping others through service predicts reduced recidivism and greater character development.[29]

Fewer social and behavioral problems are predicted in teens when they are helping family and strangers. At the end of two years, helping behavior toward family and strangers was predictive of fewer problem behaviors such as aggression and delinquency; results for friends were mixed.[30] This finding is not surprising. Studies conducted in the 1990s showed that the third of adolescents who identified their primary motive as helping others were three times happier than those who lacked such motives.[31]

Adults

One study in 1998 found that those who volunteered for one hundred hours or more were approximately 30 percent less likely to experience limitations in physical functioning when compared with nonvolunteers or those volunteering fewer hours per year. This finding remained valid even after adjusting for smoking, exercise, social connections, paid employment, health status, baseline functional limitations, socioeconomic status, and demographics.[32]

Older Adults

A study published in 2013 included 1,100 older adults aged 51–91. Subjects were interviewed about their volunteering and had their blood pressure checked in 2006, with a follow-up interview four years later in 2010. Those subjects who did volunteer work for at least 200 hours (an estimated four hours per week) in the year before their 2006 interview were 40 percent less likely than nonvolunteers to have developed hypertension four years later. This finding implies that four hours of volunteerism per week is a good idea for those who are older and have the time. The researchers suggested that this impact was due to the stress-reducing effects of being both active and altruistic.[33] This study counters any claims that volunteering has effects on mental health and mood but not on medical conditions.

THE DIGNITY AND PEACE IN GIVE AND GLOW LIVING

Wellness is only one piece of Give and Glow living. Dignity is another. Human beings have an inherent dignity and worth simply by being members of our species, however undignified they might behave. But in addition, each of us does make decisions that can add to a second form of dignity that is based on how we conduct ourselves. This second form of dignity requires us to do more than simply be human. *This is the dignity that is associated with Give and Glow living. It is the dignity of pure love, of carrying yourself with a nonviolent and kindly heart.*

This second form of dignity has been measured across all cultures and over the centuries by the extent to which we abide by the Golden Rule. Sometimes this Golden Rule is stated in the minimal terms of merely not doing anything that causes harm: "Do not do unto others as you would not have them do unto you." In the minimalist form, we use our minds to imagine things that we would not like to experience, and that we, therefore, do not want to inflict on others. In the *idealist form, we imagine all the wonderful things we can do to help others.* When we use our imaginations and energies to make the life of our neighbor better by following the Golden Rule in its positive form—"Do unto others as you'd have done unto you"—our lives improve in the process.

The following cluster of statements illustrate the Golden Rule—the first several in its minimal "do no harm" form and the last two in its idealist "do good" form. All great traditions include both, but the idealist version is the spiritual and moral formation that we strive for and from which we flourish in kindness:

- Buddhism: Hurt not others in ways that you yourself would find hurtful. *(Udana-Varga* 5.18*)*
- Confucianism: Surely it is the maxim of loving-kindness: Do not unto others that which you would not have them do unto you. *(Analects* 15.23*)*

- Islam: No man is a true believer unless he desireth for his brother that which he desireth for himself. *(Azizullah, Hadith 150)*
- Taoism: Regard your neighbor's gains as your own gain and your neighbor's loss as your own loss. *(T'ai Shang Kan Ying P'ien)*
- Zoroastrianism: That nature alone is good which refrains from doing unto another whatsoever is not good for itself. *(Dadistan-i-dinik, 94:5)*
- Brahmanism: This is the sum of duty: do naught unto others which would cause you pain if done to you. *(Mahabharata 5,1517)*
- Jain: A man should treat all creatures in the world as he himself would like to be treated. *(Wisdom of the Living Religions, #69, I:II:33)*
- Christianity: "Love the Lord your God with all your heart, and with all your soul, and with all your mind." This is the greatest and first commandment. And a second is like it: "You shall love your neighbor as yourself." On these two commandments hang all the law and the prophets. (Matt. 22:37–40)

Why does the Golden Rule exist in literally every culture that has ever taken root in human history? Over time, its minimalist form keeps the peace, and its idealist or positive form allows us all to truly live better. The positive formulation of the Golden Rule, "do unto others," is *the greatest self-help formula ever devised*. When the moral conscience is positive and clear, it closes the gap between how we should live and how we do live. There is always at least some gap between Golden Rule dignity and our real lives, which means that we need to show forbearance and forgiveness in a world of imperfection.

Inner peace derives in part from having a clean heart and mind that abides in Pure Unlimited Love. Yes, we all do things that we regret, and even a few things that we regret very deeply. When plagued with the resulting feelings of guilt and inner turbulence, the road back to inner peace must be paved with self-forgiveness and building a life based on service to others.

Our hope for inner peace comes in part from living as best we can by the positive version of the Golden Rule. Once we get a feel for the giver's glow and develop habits of kindness—out of "acting as if" or because of good role models, communities, and being intentionally raised for kindness—the love of neighbor becomes a flow state. We get into the flow of the emotional and spiritual energy of kindness and sometimes even feel that we have left time and place behind. This is such a wonderful feeling that we want to abide in it. For "Give and Glow" people, the problem of "do no harm" disappears, but we still need to be careful to respect the autonomy and self-determination of those we help.

The most obvious path to peaceful happiness lies in consistent actions that brighten up those around us; as a byproduct, we shift our emotional state in the direction of joy and tranquility. *The tension between self and other evaporates*, and we are left in a world where *the distinction between our good and another's fades, at least somewhat*. We never find happiness when we settle for selfishness. A person can be loved and served by millions, but until they become a source of loving kindness, they will not find inner peace.

To Whom Shall We Give?

While we should be kind to everyone we encounter day and night—knowing that everyone has struggles of which we are unaware—we cannot realistically give all our time, energy, and possessions and expect to care for self and family responsibly. No one can give to everyone. We must prioritize our kind giving in everyday life between three spheres: the mix of all humanity, the near and dear, and the neediest. These spheres compete for our moral attention, and all are proper areas for giving.

As a scientist-philosopher, I am not aware of any thinker who has tried to prioritize in any detail how the obligations among these spheres play out. Such a task is impossible. People are unique, and no inflexible ordering of loves would be applicable. In general, however, there should be some basic principle of symmetry among personal love, love of the remote, and love of the neediest. The spheres are related. No kind giver can love those near and dear but ignore or detest outsiders.

While we cannot give equally to all, we can pay special attention to those who, by accidents of time, place, or circumstance are brought into closer connection with us, as though by a sort of biological destiny. This includes people who are part of our lives through biology, extended family, friendships, and close communities or neighborhoods. Family values matter. We should not focus on humanity as a whole to the extent that we ignore those who are nearest, like family and friends. Yet we must also avoid being so centered on the nearest that humanity no longer seems to matter.

The sphere of personal ethics is characterized by special relationships. Its moral texture is defined by partiality, unique obligations, and proximity over extended periods of time; we know one another, often deeply. Marriage, parental love, filial love, and friendship are considered special relationships.

In all great religious and philosophical traditions, particular and exclusive forms of love in special relationships are not invalid but are appropriately held within a wider context of universal love. No moral calculus dictates an exact balance between love for those near and dear and love for the person who is most needy and/or distant. We can only conclude that universal love for humanity should never be eclipsed by special relations. This does not mean that we should sacrifice the kids' education to donate to famine relief. We do owe our children an opportunity, provided they wish to use it meaningfully.

A second sphere is occupied by the neediest, whether near or far. The neediest, whoever and wherever they are, have a powerful moral pull on us. They may lack the basics on a hierarchy of needs that includes food and water, basic medical and caregiver support, and a simple roof over their heads. We see them on the busy city sidewalks and streets from Manhattan to Bangalore. People feel special callings or embark on missions to alleviate their suffering. This calling, exemplified by Mother Teresa and Dr. Paul Farmer, often connects with all humanity but focuses on an identifiable constituency with special needs. Some caring individuals who respond to those needs may even be able to organize large numbers of inspired followers to expand their reach.

The near and dear can also be the neediest, such as when a caregiver must look after a spouse with Alzheimer's or Parkinson's disease, or when a parent stays home to look after young children. No one should be directly and personally involved in tending to all the remote neediest while being unkind or inattentive to those in the family or local community. Sometimes, we do our best for those who are far away by donating a little extra money to a charity, support organization, or faith community.

BURNOUT

Kind giving doesn't wear us out unless we overdo it. We all have physical and mental limits and finding a balance is important. So, Give and Glow but know that no one can do this well and joyfully if they feel that they are running on empty. We can all become depleted and forget as we are busy contributing to the lives of others that sometimes we need to slow down and learn to say no. We all need to be replenished, we all have physical bodies, and we need to take time to care for ourselves.

The glow of giving does fill us with meaning and energy and joy, yet every successful long-term giver feels the need to step back to connect with nature or playfulness in whatever form that fits. Mahatma Gandhi loved to take time out to weave and seemed to get into a meditational flow state that greatly replenished him. Winston Churchill would return to his beloved Chartwell, a country house in Southeast England, to lay bricks and paint the lovely scenery as a way to reconnect with his soul even as bombs were falling on London. (He was actually often out on the streets of London with everyday people during the Nazi bombing raids.) Jesus of Nazareth took time to step away from his remarkable healing ministry and retreat into the hills.

These round-the-clock givers needed to step back from it all, take their superhero capes off, and breathe deeply to stay aligned with their destinies.

There is a quote widely attributed to Abraham Lincoln, who struggled with melancholy, a deep sadness that often hung over him. He said, "When I do good I feel good; when I do bad I feel bad, and that's my religion."[34]

The glow of goodness is made of kindness, and kindness heals the world.

Tips for Giving and Glowing

- Help one person every day. Stick with this practice, especially when you're having a bad day.
- Remember the kindness. While the act of helping is vital, how much kindness was there? That is how you will be remembered.

- Draw on your talents and strengths. People tend to continue helping others when they are doing things that showcase their skills. *But you can also try something new.*
- Contact groups whose interests you share. If you think you are alone in your passion for a particular cause, think again. There are countless organizations looking for people who want to help.
- Create a helping network. Once you identify an individual or a group that you feel called to help, get involved right away. Invite your friends to come with you and be part of a little network of helping.
- Try something else if you do not find your activity gratifying.
- Take care of yourself. The typical volunteer in America helps others in organized venues for about two hours a week. If you already work in a profession that involves high levels of giving, maybe you should work toward just getting more rest and balance in your life.
- Cultivate new and deeper friendships with fellow helpers and acknowledge and celebrate what you are all doing.

My Morning Meditation

One day I was scheduled to visit the state prison in Grafton, Ohio, to talk—and *lovingly listen*—to a new prisoner who was considered tough and dangerous. In my morning meditation, well before heading out on the road to the west side of Cleveland, I focused on my friends from the prison—the prisoners I spoke to a few times a month as a volunteer. These prisoners were lifers, and I would listen to them speak of their journeys. Some of them were clearly responsible for terrible deeds and regretted them. Some grew up in hard environments. I could often sympathize with their narratives. But even when I could not side with the narrative of their lives, I could be empathetic and listen without judgment.

In addition to listening, part of my volunteer work involved teaching new inmates how to farm—helping them learn gardening skills, which were mostly foreign to the men I worked with. Grafton had a prison farm, where the inmates grew vegetables for several other prisons in Ohio, so it was important that the farmers knew what they were doing. Shortly after starting the farm, staffers realized that the gardener-prisoners seemed to be happier and more fulfilled, and prison violence dropped considerably.

In my meditation that morning, I pictured myself listening to the new prisoner's story and then I envisioned what I would say to him while helping him learn to grow vegetables. Because I had rehearsed this in my mind, and also in my heart, things went really well that afternoon. Ultimately, this prisoner developed a real green thumb.

The Full Wheel of Love in the Path of Giving and Glowing

The ten forms of love are so much easier to talk about than "love" itself because they transpose love into everyday experiences of celebration, compassionate care, forgiveness, attentive listening, "carefrontation," helpfulness, loyalty, respect, mirth, and creativity. These are variations on the theme of love as called for by human circumstances. I will only present all ten forms of love here, and in subsequent chapters re-present several of the forms that seem to be most pertinent to that specific path.

1. The Way of Celebration

I have managed many groups of mostly younger volunteers in both Cleveland and New York. My goal is to help them get the optimal benefits by meeting with them every couple of weeks to debrief over coffee or a small recognition event. Volunteering in small groups forms a community and allows people to express the meaning they are finding in giving with kindness. I like to ask the group, usually no more than eight or nine individuals, to share their most uplifting moments and any obstacles they encountered. In these groups I ask them not to be critical but simply to ask helpful questions and to respond to their peers with empathy and support. The work and bonding these people are doing calls for a celebration. We don't whoop it up. We typically have a celebratory ice cream or perhaps a cake. But these simple acknowledgments are more than enough for the group to feel recognized and welcome. It also allows participants to debrief a bit and discuss why they find their volunteering is so meaningful. This cuts down any attrition, which might otherwise be more of a problem.

2. The Way of Compassion

Kindness is having that daily approach to life that shows a "gentle curiosity" about others, as Dr. Trilling reminds me. It is not a big deal until we can't find it. Empathy is a little more complicated because we have to learn how to listen effectively and reflect that back. Compassion is a specialized form of empathy in the context of suffering and includes a willingness to alleviate that suffering to the extent possible. Compassion is in this latter sense an activity to conclude a person's suffering. Of course, one has to understand how a person is suffering, and the best way to find out is to ask a simple question: Hey, are you suffering? If so, how? And what might I be able to do to help you out?

Kindness in the simple sense means acknowledging someone and showing some interest or concern about them. Empathy is about connecting with their lives with a desire to gain understanding. Compassion is more powerful because it is a deeply affective empathic presence in the context of suffering, and includes a willingness to alleviate that suffering to the extent possible.

3. The Way of Forgiveness

Forgiveness is how we give to others who feel that they have done wrong. We are all imperfect, and I am a believer in what the AA members refer to as "the spirituality of imperfection." No relationship lasts long if we are looking for perfection.

When I first arrived in Cleveland, I volunteered a half day a week and continued this for twenty years to provide respite for the primary family caregivers of persons with dementia. Forgiving is a big part of kind caregiving. A person with dementia, for instance, will do all kinds of aggravating things that may cause caregivers to react. I once saw an elderly man scream and curse at his wife because she was asking him how to open the car door. Hearing his angry words from a few yards away, I walked over to the car in the parking lot and tried to calm this gentleman down. He was really a nice fellow, but he could not bring himself to forgive his wife for her forgetfulness. It was a big imposition on his life.

I helped her out of the car and spoke with him as we went together through the clinic doorway. "People who are deeply forgetful just can't help themselves. We have to accept them as they are and still love them." This caregiver went on to do some dementia care training programs with the respite time I provided over several months. He learned how to forgive his wife for being forgetful and dependent on him and became an exemplary caregiver.

4. The Way of Listening

Sometimes, people just need a witness—a shoulder to cry on or someone who shows enough curiosity and interest in their life journey to lend an attentive ear. Giving can be as simple—and profound—as lending an ear. Listening is multidimensional and conveys a sense of caring. It is deeper than hearing because it requires us to fully appreciate the information being taken in, and to reflect this back to the one we are giving to. Listening well is clearly a way of expressing love. Remember, when the security and well-being of another is as real and meaningful to us as our own, and sometimes more so, we love that person. Listening is among the most obvious manifestations of love. It is said that "God" loves us all because this Supreme Being listens to our prayer and supplications and answers them only when the time is right.

5. The Way of "Carefrontation"

When I was chair of the Committee on Students at Case Western Medical School, "Jake" (not his real name), one of our many brilliant students, was a bit of a joker. Before entering medical school, he'd worked as a shock jock—a radio host who expresses opinions in deliberately provocative and sometimes somewhat offensive ways. He was quite talented, but in a medical environment, he needed to learn to tone this down. Sometimes the gap between where students are before med school and where they need to get to in terms of virtues and character strengths is pretty wide.

Jake was in my office because he was in trouble for some inappropriate humor. Realizing his behavior could get him kicked out of med school, he came through the office door sheepishly, having been sent my way by one of the vice deans. I'd witnessed Jake be remarkably compassionate in the clinical setting, and I knew he had the potential to be a truly great healer, which he turned out to be.

"Jake, let's talk for a while," I said. "I am okay with humor. I love to help people laugh too. But not at anyone's expense, and I never want to offend. I have to be careful of my integrity and identity. We all do. In this building, you are not a shock jock. Here, you are a compassionate healer, and the two don't mix." We spoke deeply about good humor and not-so-good humor, discussed examples, and after a few hours, he had one of those "Come to the Light" moments. We continued to discuss this matter biweekly for the better part of a semester.

Jake breathed a sigh of relief knowing that I was going to support him, which I did. Had I simply reprimanded him, Jake might have left school—or been kicked out. But he graduated. To this day, many years later, I still get emails and cards from Jake. To paraphrase one, "Dr. Post, you taught me that carefrontation works so much better than confrontation. Carefrontation changed my life and saved my career. Now I am a successful compassionate physician mindful in everything I say to patients and peers."

I had the privilege of learning to use the word "carefrontation" from my great friend M. Scott Peck, MD, who invented it. He received his medical degree from Case Western many years before I arrived there, but we appreciated one another and carried on a lively correspondence by phone and letter when we finally met. We were both writing on the theme of higher love, and he reminded me that "confrontation" was a negative word, one that could be replaced by something better. As he suggested to me kindly and effectively, maybe you should include in your writings an approach to love that is less 'soft' when it has to be. He suggested "the risk of carefrontation," a concept in his book *The Road Less Traveled*. I took his recommendation with gratitude, and have included it in my Wheel of Love. "Scotty" was a psychiatrist, and every psychiatrist needs to rely on "carefrontation" to be successful with patients.

6. The Way of Helpfulness

The smallest acts of kind giving can have lasting effects. Karen cleans up the offices in our halls and does a fabulous job. She is very diligent and meticulous, always a sign that she finds her work meaningful and even a calling. She is a Give and Glow role model for me, and she never seeks attention. Her humility is exemplary. In China the symbol for the helper is water, because it always goes to the lowest level and it is rarely much noticed, but makes a huge contribution. One day, I saw that she was having a hard time with a heavy trash can, so I walked over and picked it up for her. She was appreciative, and we still have a special bond based on that one minor gesture. I always say hello to her in the hallways. It makes my day. And I make a small donation to her favorite charity. I worry that we need to do more to celebrate her, and so sometimes I bring in a gift, and always say hello warmly in the mornings. I always thank her for her helpfulness because if you feel grateful to someone it is good to say so.

7. The Way of Loyalty

I knew a young student who was suffering because her boyfriend of five years had left her. She felt her whole life crumbling, and she seemed depressed. One day I saw her in the hallway crying and invited her to my office. I just listened and finally said that the boyfriend was losing a wonderful person in his life. I became a source of loyalty for her as a mentor and knew that this was the best expression of love that I could offer. She needed a sense of security by having me stick with her in support. There are countless studies of how the insecurity of relationships in modern culture contributes to anxiety and depression, and even to suicide. We need to provide stability as a counterpoint. We all need that stability and trust.

8. The Way of Respect

The word "respect" comes from the Latin *respectare*, which means to look twice, or to re-look. When we respect someone, we stop to take their perspectives seriously. This takes humility. When giving with kindness, we need to let those we are helping see that we are being caring, attentive, and nonjudgmental in our thoughts and actions. It is not good for anyone if we try to be helpful but are also being disrespectful. Each person is unique, and we need to honor and appreciate them. Each adds to our life together. Like flowers, each adds to a garden. I always respect the choices of volunteers to be engaged with a cause that they select in a way that they wish, sometimes drawing on their skill sets or sometimes they want to do something they have not done before.

9. The Way of Mirth

Actor and comedian Bob Hope lived to be one hundred. What made him so great? His mirth and laughter brought smiles to millions, including troops stationed in war zones across the world over seven decades. He always had time for a quiet moment with a wounded soldier, no matter how tired he might be from a long flight or a busy schedule. Bob Hope also spent a lot of time in nursing homes and special care units with deeply forgetful people. His mirthfulness, his natural joy, carried over to them. And often after singing a song that they could easily recall from their generation, he would share a few jokes and people across the room would all smile and laugh.

As famous and rich as he was, Bob Hope saw the need to show his love of humanity by giving of himself—by encouraging others to laugh. Love can be expressed in levity, and angels fly because of their lightness. It is hard to imagine loving someone you can't laugh with, at least a little. Laughter frees us from anxiety or despair. When we laugh, the ego self seems to disappear. Our worries just go out the window. We forget about the weight of life and in that brief moment experience a new beginning. Humor distracts us from the constant march and demands of chronological time. Mirth is one of the most wonderful gifts we can give. With discretion, I try to help people laugh a bit to regain their lightness of being with positive good humor.

The 2025 World Happiness Report ranks the United States twenty-fourth in the world, largely attributed to a breakdown of social ties and communities. Especially post-COVID, giving has not gotten back to where it was. We need to get back to more giving, and we need to do this with loving-kindness. My own observation is that we need to remember how to laugh.

10. The Way of Creativity

The Hindus teach that the Supreme Being is characterized by love, creativity, and freedom. While working with a group of volunteers one day, I overheard Sheri lamenting that she was a poor interior decorator. She didn't have a lot of money but wanted to make her home feel and look cozier. Janice, a younger woman in the group, piped up and said she loves to decorate on a shoestring budget and would be happy to help. She said that she could start with items that Sheri already owned and then fill in the blanks with pieces from thrift stores. The next time the group met, Sheri was thrilled with the results, saying she never could have imagined someone could be so creative with so little—and so generous and giving with their time and energy. Creativity is one way that we exist in the image of the divine, and it is as such a sacred activity.

Concluding Thoughts

There is nothing better than being a kind giver experiencing Give and Glow radiance. St. Paul wrote that "each of you must give as you have made up your mind, not reluctantly or under compulsion, for God loves a cheerful giver" (2 Cor. 9:7). I meditated on this verse a lot as a boy, and it has stayed with me. I hope it stays with you. Be a kind, loving, and cheerful giver.

CHAPTER 2

The Second Path: May You Heal with Kindness

> "She opens her mouth with wisdom, and the teaching of kindness is on her tongue."
>
> —Proverbs, 31:26

As we come into this world with our first breath, we are completely open. There is no judgment, no preformed sense of self or other. We are, in that moment, pure love. Before words, before rational thought, our visceral experience penetrates deeply. We sense the complete love of a parent holding us just after birth as it flows into our every fiber of being. And if there is fear, worry, or rejection, this too is felt in full measure.

As we grow up, the shaping power of this unspoken experience remains, informing our sense of being. Kindness is part of this unspoken language that reaches our innermost being. Kindness signifies that we are seen. That, in a given moment, we are acknowledged and accepted as we are. And kindness is important because, whether a brief or long exchange, kindness touches the heart and has the power to heal.

WHAT IS KINDNESS?

There is nothing fancy about kindness. *Kindness* is a consistent, low-key, and simple form of love. It is like water, which we cannot do without. Water is the symbol of humility in Asian cultures. It never seeks the highest levels in a landscape. Rather, it naturally and humbly gravitates to fill up the lower spaces. For the most part, many of us take water for granted. But like flowers, we die without it.

Maybe kindness has become a little less normal in everyday American life, so it is no wonder that people have more mental health problems per capita than in decades gone by. Maya Angelou picked up on this cultural shift: "I am truly grateful . . . for appreciating love—for knowing that it exists in a world so rife with vulgarity, with brutality and violence . . . And I'm grateful to know it exists in me, and I'm able to share it with so many people."[35] She was a remarkably kind women and this brought much success to her life. I once gave a speech at Wake Forest University in Winston-Salem, North Carolina, where she resided as a distinguished poet. Afterward, we had tea together in her home. Dressed in an African tribal gown, she asked me, "Stephen, that Pure Unlimited Love idea, do you really believe in it?"

"I do because it is all we have to stay hopeful," I responded.[36]

St. Paul described love as kind, patient, gentle, never boastful or self-inflated, and not hot-tempered.[37] Gentleness is the softness of life, and it encourages states of inner and outer peace. But it is only soft in part. Kindness is also a core character *strength*. Gandhi associated kindness with courage and fearlessness and understood nonviolence to require these strengths.

The Athenians believed kindness and gentleness were essential to civilization itself. Kindness was the refusal to inflict pain or harshness, and it conveyed nonviolence and a willingness to do good and to heal. Lao Tzu, the founder of Chinese Taoism, in his classic *The Tao Te Ching*, emphasized that while water is the softest and most yielding things, it can carve even the hardest rocks (verse 78). The principle is that kindness can overcome hardness. The word "kindness" conveys a commitment to regard all people equally. In kindness there is no exclusion. Kindness transcends distinctions that might otherwise separate us: class, race, religion, ethnicity, education, gender, poverty, sexual identity, and cognitive and physical disabilities. Kindness is undeterred by the dehumanization and othering that pervades our world. Kindness touches those deeper dimensions of heart and mind where another person is recognized and felt to be of profound value.

Kindness is a setting of the heart and an underlying state of being. It is the powerful and empowering backbone of all lasting, meaningful, and good relationships and is apparent in details such as tone of voice, facial expression, empathic response, and degree of presence and attentiveness. The word "kindness" focuses the mind on the small details of our interactions with the world. Rather than just passing others by, we *see* facial expressions, *hear* tone of voice, and *make space* for a listening pause. Kindness is inwardly cultivated and requires a steady inner state that overcomes external pressures to abandon it in times of haste, stress, and adversity.

Kindness conveys to everyone we encounter on our path that they have dignity, worth, and intrinsic beauty. Kindness is not an abstract "love for humanity" far and wide but a concrete, immediate way of engaging the world right where we are. We are each the right person in the right place at the right time to be kind.

Kindness emerges in humility, or an accurate sense of self and its place in an equal-regarding mindset. When we have humility, we leave space in the room for others to be fully present, to speak without disturbance, and to be considered in their dignity. We refuse to fill the room with our ego. This brings inner peace because it frees us from the burden of self-promotion and making things up about out personal achievements.

Simple politeness and good manners can be expressions of kindness. Sometimes kindness takes the form of a "please," "thank you," or "you're welcome." These are not big things, but they are the stuff of a well-lived life. But sometimes having manners is just a way of asserting classism and superiority, so we do not think of politeness as being especially deep. Kindness is deeper than politeness but hopefully underlies it.

During my twenty years of teaching the ethics of compassion at Case Western School of Medicine, I was often inspired by Dr. Robert Haynie, then dean of students and a good friend. He was a fabulous role model for kindness. Bob often spoke of the famous Dr. Joseph M. Foley, a mutual friend and chairman of the Department of Neurology. Despite Dr. Foley's busy schedule, he dedicated a day a week to rounding with the medical students. As a former student of Dr. Foley, Dr. Haynie recalled these events fondly:

> Dr. Foley insisted that we stop in front of each patient's door, pausing to unclutter our minds from the immediately preceding patient encounter. We entered each patient's room only after knocking and asking permission. Dr. Foley would pull up a chair, sit down, and take the patient's hands, asking, "How can I and my colleagues make this a better day for you?" We were reminded by Dr. Foley to observe the patient with care and listen attentively. We were shocked when he introduced us as colleagues before he took a history.

On one occasion, a patient was rather surprised and said, "I would love to have a glass of iced tea with lemon!" At that point, Dr. Foley left the room and returned with the tea. The patient smiled and informed us that she had been hospitalized multiple times, but no one had ever done anything so kind for her. Dr. Foley then went to work masterfully, taking a history and performing a neurological exam as if he were conducting a symphony orchestra. Dr. Foley's rounds consistently left us with a sense of self-worth and a desire to emulate the kindness we had witnessed.[38]

The suffering of hospital patients is usually obvious. But most people are hurting and suffering to some extent for some deep reason that we know nothing about so we must always be kind because being anything less does a lot of hidden damage. Kindness is the minimal expression of love, requires no great training, and is appreciated by everyone, especially those feeling a bit empty inside or maybe burned out from a long day on the job. This is when a simple smile or the thoughtful action of opening the door for someone has the power to lift the soul to the heights of heaven.

THE KINDNESS SPECIALIST

Meditating on a bench on the Brooklyn Heights Promenade as a young man fresh out of college, I looked through the employment section of the *New York Post* thinking that I would do something that was of service to others. I found a listing for a dialysis technician at the Manhattan Dialysis Center in midtown on 30th street. It was 1974, and kidney machines were still new and a challenging ordeal for patients, although they were free for everyone thanks to the US Congress. Within weeks I was numbing up the skin over the bovine graft in countless wrist veins before slipping in a butterfly needle and watching the blood flow red through a clear rubber line.

I kept a journal about the human side of the patients' experiences so I could connect a little better with them. I asked them what was hardest for them about dialysis, what they feared most about getting hooked up, how they coped, and if they felt that they were being treated kindly. I observed that some were treated with kindness, but others were not. The ones who were treated insensitively, inconsiderately, and coldly, in contrast to those who were treated kindly, were by my casual observation about twice as likely to stop showing up for their appointments at some point as the months passed, at which point I assumed that they had passed away.

I was determined to treat everyone kindly, like VIPs in a fancy hotel, by focusing on the little things, like tone of voice, listening well, communicating clearly, and making sure everyone had something to read. The number of patients leaving for good dropped. The director, Dr. Norman Dean, complimented me and wanted me to think about becoming a physician one day.

The staff noticed that kindness was having an effect. They asked me to spend more time just talking kindly with patients. From then on, I was allowed to spend less time on the technical aspects of the work with patients and more time serving as "the kindness specialist." I succeeded with lots of quiet listening punctuated by tasteful dad jokes that got people laughing. Experts say laughter boosts the immune system by lowering stress, slows pulse rate, lowers blood pressure, and helps get the mind off suffering.[39]

I became someone who patients called on to sit down by their big chairs and steady them, often by just listening, which was mostly all it took.

Arrogance Versus Humility

As a youth, I knew many kind people. Those kind people around me were always humble. They made equal space for all, including self.

As a youth, I was also sometimes bullied. Most of the people in my school came from families with more money than mine, from nicer and bigger homes, and were better educated from a much younger age. It all added up to some of my cohorts feeling superior to me.

When being unkind, people are usually also being arrogant. Arrogance is the opposite of humility. Arrogance can take the form of snobbery and appear as derisive humor or subtle "insider" exclusivity. Arrogant people might not notice you. Or they might humiliate you and try to make you feel small, as if you have no gifts or talents that are worthwhile. After a while, you might begin to feel de-dignified. Arrogance creates walls between "them" and "us," which are constructed to de-dignify through language and facial expression. We all have biases that drive us away from being the humble healers we may aspire to be, but snobbery is an extreme form of arrogance.

Arrogance is powerful enough to destroy truth by characterizing lying as a mark of boldness. Lies, if told frequently enough, will eventually be believed. We hear partisans who do not think twice about distorting the truth. Pontius Pilate found Jesus guilty of no crime but nevertheless asserted, *"Quid est veritas?"* or "What is truth?"[40] The sincere commitment to honesty begins with the humble individual who knows that they are not more important than truth and that they do not possess absolute truth—because no human being does.

Arrogance is exhausting because we have to defend our false, indefensible superiority. Having to defend an untruth is tiring and stressful and precludes being one's authentic self. It is the antithesis of true inner peace.

We are all imperfect. Humility means that we accept our imperfections as we accept the imperfections of others, thus ending harsh judgments. Without humility we cannot admit mistakes, apologize, and try again. There is no real love without humility and no real healing. *But there is joy and kindness in humility.*

Arrogance and unkindness are linked as the sources of so much unnecessary stress, suffering, desperate emptiness, and illness. But kindness heals the world and everyone in it one by one, including the healers themselves. Kindness is the light of the everyday world.

The most significant contemporary conceptualization of humility is found in *Character Strengths and Virtues: A Handbook and Classification,* the key text of positive psychology, where kindness and humility are closely linked. Key features of humility identified in this handbook include an accurate sense of one's abilities and achievement, a nondefensive willingness to see oneself, including strengths and limitations, an openness to new ideas, keeping a low focus on the self, and affirming the value of all people and the different ways they contribute to our world. A self-disparaging or contemptuous attitude toward the self is to be avoided, as is an overestimation of the value of self in relation to others.[41]

There are various humility scales that are used in research, most of which include items along the lines of these:

1. I would rather be always right than always kind.
2. My ideas are almost always the right ones.
3. I'd trust my own knowledge about most things and tend not to turn to others for different perspectives.
4. I have a hard time changing my opinions even when someone suggests I may be wrong.
5. I revise my important beliefs when new contradictory facts comes to light.
6. I often gain deep insight from others.

7. I enjoy being exposed to the different ways of thinking about important topics.
8. Even when I disagree with others, I can recognize that they have some good points to make based on their experiences.
9. When someone contradicts my most important beliefs, it does not feel like a personal attack.
10. I tend to respect others, and even appreciate them, when they ask me to reconsider my opinions by pointing out the need for cultural humility, even if I disagree with them in important ways.

EXCHANGING WORDS

Why the word "kindness" in particular? We use it because "kindness" is a simple word. People know what it means and use it without any embarrassment. It is not foreboding or intimidating but uncomplicated and easy to understand. It needs no special revelation, no esoteric sources, and no rare insights. It is refreshingly unifying because we all know what it means to be a little kinder, and we know when we fall short. Much as I use the word "love," people may ask, "So what kind of love are we talking about?" Kindness carries no such confusion. Sometimes I use the expression "loving-kindness," which is central in Jewish theology.

Kindness is related to empathy but much less complicated. Empathy requires listening attentively as another person tells their story and expresses their emotions. Empathy requires us to pause, observe, listen in-depth, and reflect back what we have heard. Empathy is informed by feeling, and without feeling there is no empathy. While it is to some degree natural, empathy requires cultivating our innate ability to pick up on the feeling states of others.

Compassion is even more complex because it builds on empathy exclusively in the context of suffering and the willingness to alleviate its source. Emerging through deep recognition of the truth of human suffering, compassion requires a willingness to be present to it. Compassion

> is unconditional; its palpable essence can be expressed in a brief exchange or over time.
>
> Compassion as a response to suffering asks us to notice the suffering in one another. It might be thought of as empathic presence that does not run away from the sounds and sights of suffering but that manages to remain attentive and responsive. Not everyone is cut out for compassion, whereas others are quite exemplary and even saintly in this virtue.

Kindness and Healing

Every human being is unique—our journeys shaped by multifaceted contours of time, place, culture, and circumstance. While each path is different, we share essential aspects of life—struggle, joy, comfort, fear, love, doubt, family, relationships. In the moments when we respond to another's humanity with a simple heart-set of kindness, we lighten their burden.

Yes, we are all healers when we are kind. Each one of us without exception is potentially a healer by virtue of our inherent humanity. No education or degree is needed. I tend to agree with the Buddha and Danish theologian Søren Kierkegaard that we are all suffering at some level. We may look happy and cheerful today, but we also fear a time when what makes us happy will disappear. And so, it's important to notice and offer kindness to everyone, even those who do not seem to be suffering.

Kindness also contributes to physical healing, a truth that was understood in Western culture until the mid-1600s, when René Descartes, "the father of modern philosophy," suggested that the mind and the body were disconnected and entirely separate. Thus, physicians in the Western medical schools where I have taught with rare exceptions hold that illness is a disorder of the biological half of the human being, and the idea that mind and emotions have much effect on disease progression is deemed unscientific. While things are evolving to a more mind-body integrated philosophy of the illness experience, most medical investigation is biological, and Descartes still rules the roost.

THE RESEARCH

Over the past few decades, we've researched kindness, and we know that kindness heals in every human context, from the family to the school to the place of worship to the simple act of giving up one's seat on the bus.

Simple kindness calms the destructive emotions and anxiety that beset almost everyone, especially in times of deep social and cultural polarization. Young adults who report having experienced parental kindness rather than emotional or physical violence have half the rates of mental and physical illness in midlife and tend to avoid alcohol or drug abuse as teens.[42] Patients who experience empathy from their physicians and nurses are more likely to continue with challenging medical treatments, share important information about their illness, and live healthy lives.[43]

At Stony Brook, we do a great deal of original research on kindness in relation to physical healing. We've discovered that kindness contributes to healing chronic illnesses, especially conditions where adherence to treatment is necessary over a very extended period, as is true with diabetes, kidney disease, heart disease, and more.

Biologically, how does kindness heal? Kindness lowers cortisol, the primary stress hormone. Cortisol is beneficial to the body in short bursts because it elevates energy and empowers the "fight-flight" response, which is good when we need to put up our dukes or run fast in the face of danger. However, if levels of cortisol are consistently high for months or even years, the cortisol will gradually convert metabolites into fatty acids, and this contributes to cardiovascular disease, or compromised blood vessels.

A study conducted in the 1990s by Redford Williams, who was then chair of the Duke University Department of Cardiology, and colleagues considered the answers to select Minnesota Multiphasic Personality Inventory (MMPI) questions—those related to rumination, anger, bitterness, resentment, and so forth—from 1950 and 1975. The researchers looked only at respondents who were aged twenty-five in 1950. Twenty percent of those who the MMPI revealed were most hostile were dead by age fifty (1975), almost all from the cardiovascular disease that results from fatty acid buildup; only 2 percent of those considered to be the least hostile were dead.

In a nutshell, if you interact with others over the years with a short fuse and are unable to forgive those who have been hurtful, you are not harming them so much as yourself. Williams even wrote a book about it: *Anger Kills*.[44]

Destructive emotions have even been associated with Alzheimer's. When angry or anxious, our elevated stress hormones cause the hippocampus—the part of the brain needed to lay down short-term memories—to shrink. A well-known prevention study showed that private spiritual activity reduced stress, enhanced kindness, and this in turn reduced susceptibility to Alzheimer's.[45]

People also heal faster because kindness reduces stress, strengthens the immune response, and fosters resilience.[46]

KINDNESS: THE SECRET TO SUCCESS

I am a little older now and have been teaching around medical schools for years. In my days at Case Western School of Medicine, I knew a wonderful neurologist named Joseph M. Foley (the same Dr. Foley mentioned on page 38), whose dad was a first-generation Irish immigrant to Boston. Joe was known for his immense humility. He went to Harvard Med before he took up his position as a medic at Omaha Beach during World War II and lived to tell the story. When he died at the age of ninety-six, his church in Cleveland Heights was full of patients and friends who all echoed a common refrain, "He was the kindest man I ever knew." That was Joe's secret to success as a human being and a physician—kindness was one of the healing tools he pulled out of his doctor's bag.

The last time I saw Joe alive was in his home the day before he died. I had just driven back to Cleveland from New York that day and had a strong intuition to visit Joe's home. Joe was not able to talk. I knew he loved Irish jokes, so I thought I'd return some of this mirthful healing kindness. Expecting no response due to his condition, I gently reminded him of some of the jokes that he had told me over the years. When I said "Joe, what's the Irish definition of hospitality?" he could not respond. But when I delivered the punchline—"You make someone feel perfectly at home while you are a' wishin' they were"—Joe cracked up laughing. He still, deep down, responded to the healing nature of kindness delivered with good-hearted humor.

Success and happiness require more than lots of achievement and recognition. Success derives from kindness and meaning, not from a jam-packed resume and the highest salary (although not surprisingly they can and often do go hand in hand). As one who has spent considerable time around dying people, I can attest that one of the regrets sometimes expressed is, "I should have been kinder, and now it is too late." Dying words, especially those that are commonly heard, are important food for thought: *Am I missing out on kindness, and as a consequence, am I missing out on life itself?*

A Healing Journey

In a famous 1926 lecture to medical students, as he grappled with the cancer that would soon take his life, Harvard Medical School physician Francis Weld Peabody affirmed (and would later publish): "One of the essential qualities of the clinician is interest in humanity, for the secret of the care of the patient is in caring for the patient."[47] Physicians, and other healers, are often present when and where kindness matters most.

The significance of kindness in caring for patients illuminates the healing power of kindness for us all. As one who directs educational programs in the "how to" of empathy and compassionate care, I see the difference this training makes in medical students as they go through our courses and start treating patients. And I am acutely aware of what the experience of being kind offers to the rest of humanity. The common ground of shared humanity, affirmed through kindness, can restore true balance, creating connection, trust, and care. As we meet one another in our day-to-day, we carry the meaning of life within us. An immediate moment of heart-to-heart connection opens the door to feelings of inner peace for those who experience solitude as loneliness, and even for those like myself, who enjoy the quiet of solitude, it surely adds meaning.

We are all healers, and in the healing, we too are healed. This experience is a journey: the time will come with the right combination of scientific and spiritual truth when each of us follows the path to healing with kindness.

The Healer's Journey looks something like this:

1. We enter a world where everything is new. We are immersed in an unfamiliar world with a language largely foreign. We

begin to form our sense of the world by what we hear, witness, and experience.
2. Without the shield of preformed judgments, experiences penetrate deeply. We begin to draw conclusions about whether the world is safe or perilous, whether we are loved or rejected. This begins to shape our understanding of expectations and values and who we will become. We grow from each experience, whether affirming or difficult. We may feel embattled as we navigate the terrain. The journey is challenging.
3. Children who are loved will learn the language of love and the expression of it, drawing from the well in their interaction with others. Children raised with negativity, fear, and discouragement find it more difficult to be caring.
4. Those capable of kindness recognize each individual—their unique experience, ideas, and goals—and relate to each one with care. This nourishes self-compassion and fosters a wellspring of caring for others. (If we take care of our children, caring for others will take care of itself.)
5. Moving through life we face responsibilities, demands, and concerns large and small. Kindness is a welcome comfort. The common ground of shared humanity, expressed through kindness, can restore balance, create connection, and trust. A moment of heart-to-heart connection opens the door to healing—for both the giver and the receiver.
6. The inevitable churn of life informs inner awareness and compassion for others. Each phase calls for new levels of growth and often prompts a renewed sense of vulnerability. Discouragement, self-doubt, losing sight of our visions: With awareness, these same events strengthen inner development, fostering compassion, deepening confidence, and forging

strength from difficulty. Feeling our own vulnerability, we can sense vulnerability in others. When we feel the unkindness of another, we can recognize their pain.

7. We are one community; so too are we endlessly diverse. Yet everyone can cultivate habits of heart that yield kindness so that each can navigate the human terrain, expressing kindness in their own authentic voice.

8. A vital part of nourishing awareness in a healer's journey is for the healer to see, acknowledge, and affirm their authentic voice—their unique being. Our inner inspiration is where we come alive; it animates our being and informs our path. It is essential to nourish that flame within. During times of difficulty, inner inspiration may seem suppressed and inaccessible. In those times, through encouragement of a trusted other or through our own reflection, we can connect with that "still small voice within."

9. Armed with knowledge of the human experience, we can serve the person before us, responding to their individual need in that moment. Without that connection, a difficult path can seem discouraging. With it, that same path yields growth and deepens confidence. From the place of inner confidence, we can truly see, and care for, another.

10. Anyone who abides in kindness is spared the harms of destructive emotions like bitterness and rumination, which we know elevate stress hormones for unhealthy periods. These hormones are good in short bursts, like running away from a snake or crocodile when you need extra energy and speed, but if left turned on for long periods due to anxiety and destructive negative emotions, these hormones do a lot of damage.

Empathic and Compassionate Healthcare

Kindness is so important and so universal that the World Health Organization has designated "compassionate care" as a worldwide goal of all medical education, and the American Academy of Medical Colleges has stressed this as a goal of US medical schools. The National Health Service (NHS) in the United Kingdom reports that healthcare is more at risk now than ever for deteriorating humanism and recommends restoring its core founding principles—kindness and compassion for the common good. This, they assert, must be at the very center of any NHS reforms. In the United States, most physicians and medical students recognize that "empathic care" and "compassionate care" are important to therapeutic outcomes. However, in one survey only 53 percent of patients and 58 percent of physicians reported that compassionate care was generally provided in the US healthcare system.[48]

The drive for human connection and "attachment" increases greatly during times of major distress and serious illness. This is intensified in the depersonalized and unfamiliar environment of the clinical setting. The presence of an empathic and compassionate clinician is a gift that can achieve much for patient healing and should therefore be considered as significant as other treatment interventions. The patient will view it as such.

Considerable research suggests that people who receive empathic care experience emotional security that promotes healing. This phenomenon is consistent with the higher cortisol levels detected in individuals who report protracted stress and the consequent slowing of wound healing, as well as vascular effects and hippocampal atrophy, which is a biological hallmark of an Alzheimer's disease diagnosis.

When clinicians are empathic, they may achieve earlier and more accurate diagnoses because patients who receive empathic care feel more emotionally safe and are more likely to divulge information. More efficient treatment planning and better patient adherence to treatment plans usually follows.

Some of our research indicates that medical students, clinicians, nurses, residents and other staff members benefit as well. Studies show that when clinicians can maintain kind care, they find practice meaningful and are more resilient. Importantly for anyone in medical education, the *Journal the American Academy of Medicine* reported in 2018 that medical students who are more empathic in medical school have lower burnout rates in residency.[49] Nearly 90 percent of physicians who report erosion in their enthusiasm for medicine attribute this loss to the ways in which financial and time pressures inhibit empathic care. Yet when clinicians are satisfied with their relationships with patients, we see reductions in professional stress, burnout, substance abuse, and suicide attempts.[50] As the motto of my Institute states it, and as approved personally by Sir John Templeton in 2003, "In the giving of self lies the unsought for discovery of a deeper self."

Caring is partly of the mind and partly of the heart in synergy, expressed through energetic presence one-to-another. If we as healers are alert to that realm, it is palpable, more real than what is conveyed in words—a felt connection person to person. Presence is not personal involvement; it is awakened awareness emerging from the resonant humanity of being. It sees no separation between self and another. It is mutual and bidirectional. It is restorative, a conduit for connection. Presence does not diminish but elevates. Conscious connection does not deplete, it enriches. Enlivened awareness of the suffering of another allows the healing force to follow.

Kindness is a channel for caring. The educated heart sees the other and responds, opening the way to connection. Unhindered by external difference, it is felt all at once. From the place of our shared humanity, kindness heals, person-to-person, heart-to-heart, soul-to-soul; the energy of healing flows, one to another.

Moving through the world with hearts and minds open to love, we see and sense the experience of another and in that moment, we connect and heal through kindness. We find inner peace in this deep meaning, because we know deep down that we are on the right track.

Humility Empowers Kindness

The world sometimes seems to reward those who shout the loudest. But humble people who are not trying to impress anyone do develop a nice reputation for doing things from the kindness of their hearts and for being humble about it as well.[51] They heal with kindness in every interaction because that is how they live meaningfully. They do well socially because they do not place themselves above other people, and they are in general more helpful to others.[52]

One of our finest students decided to enter the field of anesthesiology. He is a wonderfully talented and humble young man and widely respected as such. He was admitted into Stanford University for his clinical residency program. When I asked why he chose to specialize in anesthesiology, his response was that the anesthesiologist is the last person patients see before going unconscious, and they never quite know if they will wake up on the other end of this. He felt a calling to reassure patients on this journey by communicating with great kindness and attentiveness—he wanted the last person they might ever see to be kind and caring. And he hoped that should they not reawaken, that they would find themselves immersed beautifully and peacefully in the light of Pure Unlimited Love.

Humility is the precondition for kindness and our saving grace because it means that others are as valuable and worth being kind to as we are. Just think for a moment about the insults and unkindness that flow between people of differing political parties who believe that their side has the only perspective worthy of consideration. Those who see things differently are demonized and even annihilated. A hideous form of arrogance is genocide, in which one political, ethnic, cultural, or racial group has so much sense of superiority that they determine to eliminate whole other groups by any means necessary and proceed to wipe them off the face of the earth.

Those who affirm dialogue and peace based on our shared humanity, such as Lincoln, Gandhi, Dr. King, and Benazir Bhutto, are so threatening to the arrogant superiors that they fall victim to the assassin's bullets. Abraham Lincoln often cited the proposition from Euclid that "two things which are equal to the same thing are equal to each other."[53] He even defined America as a nation "dedicated to the proposition that all men are created equal."[54] This meant that if fully realized, all Americans would have equal rights and opportunities. He used the phrase during the Civil War as a moral imperative of fighting to abolish slavery and to reaffirm in clearer terms the nation's commitment to equality. It is humility that most helps us cultivate kindness, empathy, and compassion.

A recent study in the *Journal of Personality Assessment* tightly links intellectual humility—the ability to recognize that you don't know everything—and kindness.[55] This and now dozens of other research articles indicate that over the past decade, intellectual humility has gone from a topic of philosophical and theological inquiry to one of well-developed scientific investigation. The science points out that those who are high in humility are aware of their own limitations.[56]

It turns out, as expected, that those who respect and appreciate the thoughts and ideas of others generally have high levels of kindness and empathy.[57] Humility is the great equalizer, freeing people from being overly concerned with elevating self over others.

Humility and kindness together make equal space in the room for others. Without humility, the self alone fills the room and crowds others out. This inflated self is not the true self, any more than it is true that the earth rather than the sun is the center of the universe around which all else orbits. The same can be said of in-groups of all kinds that tend to think they are more perfect than out-groups, when in fact the features that they believe make them better never hold against logical criticism. It usually turns out that the people in that "othered" group are just as creative, intelligent, motivated, and gifted as "we" are. This is the logic of equality.

A Big Tip: Stop, Look, Listen

In a world where we can be anything, we can first of all be kind. Being kind is so much better than always trying to be right. It can be valuable to take time to pause just a moment for kindness at work, in school, at home, and wherever we find ourselves. To heal with kindness, we need to step out of the rush and slow down enough to be more mindful of those around us and let community form.

Stop, Look, and Listen

Several of my physician colleagues here at Stony Brook came up with an approach to increasing empathy and compassion on the clinical floor. We came up with "Stop, Look & Listen (SLL)" as the key to kindness. Generating a kind and gentle curiosity about the people around you anywhere and anytime makes people feel at ease, leading to more productive and better communication throughout the day. It avoids judging, blaming, reacting, criticizing, or de-dignifying others.[58]

In its full description, SLL begins with a **Stop**, what the poets call a caesura, or clearing pause. The pause can be in any moment and place: in a restaurant, the hallway, the grocery store, or during any experience.

Then follows **Look**, by which we intentionally and nonjudgmentally notice the visual details of others. It is the same level of attentiveness that one might see in an art class at the museum, where students are asked what they see in a painting and are always surprised by all they miss. We have to notice details. This is not observation alone but also an understanding of what our observation evokes. It takes practice, but we can notice potential discomforts and ask people if they could use some help.

Then follows **Listen**. In this phase, we do more than hear words. We comprehend the meaning that undergirds their words by reflecting back what we have just heard: "Let me just repeat what I think you said, but correct me if I have this wrong." This assures people you are taking them seriously.

Anyone can use the SLL technique. During a busy day, we can take time to Stop, Look, and Listen to those who are right before us in the moment by tuning out distracting extraneous thoughts and focusing on the face we see or the words we hear. The practice of

SLL helps restore meaning to our daily exchange with others, fostering well-being and flourishing. It communicates to children, colleagues, friends, and everyone we encounter that we are interested in them as people who are fully worthy of connection and kindness. We not only enrich their experience but our own.

SLL creates space to step back into the moment and respond well, even amid pressure and anxious turmoil. Cultivating kindness in everyday practice, we complete our day with no regrets for not having been a little kinder.

Tips for Healing with Kindness

- Slow down, even stop, then look and listen with care. It's hard to heal on the run.
- Be present. In our haste, those around us do not sense our presence at the emotional level. Start with a few words of gentle curiosity. How's that daughter of yours? Did you see the Guardians yesterday? How about those Cavs?
- Don't interrupt. Count seven seconds after you speak a word so that the person you are healing has plenty of time to say something. Maybe their words are on the tip of their tongues, but they are a little slow to respond for cultural or other reasons.
- Be patient. Patience is a big part of having a healing presence. Patience is the mean between rushing and being idle. If people could just be a bit more patient and have some forbearance, connectivity would increase exponentially. Healing is mostly about connections.
- Rely on others and call upon them to be helpful. Healing happens in the quiet of a trusting friendship, but it is also a team endeavor. No one alone has all the answers.

- Invite people into small circles of trust around the coffee table. Let them discuss the human and emotional aspects of their lives. A Reflection Round is a circle of trust—a safe haven for the emotional, relational, and in the broadest sense of the term, "spiritual" aspects of their interactions. It is a circle that requires an empathic, attentive, and focused approach to dialogue. Just do this with your friends if they are willing.
- Respond, don't react. There is a big difference. People who react tend to be absolutist and dismissive, and they don't control their emotions well. They will say things that they are sorry about later on and wish they could take back. To respond is to have enough emotional control and to be kind and affirming of the person despite disagreement.
- Be open to different perspectives, rather than judging them harshly or unfairly. Just figure that they have a perspective of their own that is different from yours. Kindness and non-judgment go hand in hand.
- Be still. Moments of silence can be very healing, especially after someone has spoken with depth.

My Morning Meditation

In the early morning, some people take a little time to chant an ancient line from fifteenth-century Japan: *Nam-myoho-renge-kyo*. I do this fairly often. This is hard to translate, but it means something like "I honor the divine resilience in us all." It assumes that we are all connected not just as biological creatures, but as all equally part of the universal mind. Meditating on our Oneness is so important because much of our culture tears us apart and polarizes us, so we forget our common or shared humanity.

I close my eyes and envision someone I love and tell them that I honor the divine in them. Then I envision someone who I know at work or in the neighborhood and also tell them that I honor them. Then I turn to an adversary and do the same. I have no enemies because those who oppose my work are all sent into my path to bring out the best in me. They are ultimately helpful to me because they allow the kind of challenges that I need to grow.

Honoring the divine in everyone, even those who are adversarial, is how I avoid the spiritual pitfall of rumination and move my mind from hostility to kindness to inner peace. It also is helpful when it comes to self-forgiveness, because I live within the energy of universal Mind and universal Love.

The Wheel of Love in Healing Kindness

The Way of Celebration

People who try to be a healing presence in their friendships, families, and communities are celebrated. Celebrations are not just times when we get loud and happy. "Celebration" comes from the Latin word *celebrare*, which means "to assemble to honor." We are honoring the divine in others and reminding them of their dignity. Honoring others is a kind and generous form of celebration.

The Way of Forgiveness

A young resident in Cleveland came into my office in tears and wanted to leave school. He'd made a grave diagnostic mistake that resulted in a patient's death. While mistakes are inevitable in any profession, the consequences of a doctor's mistake can be irreversible, affecting patients, family, and staff. In many ways, becoming a doctor is a process of learning to live with all the dozens of mistakes they will make.

"Rev. Martin Luther King Jr. said that those who make no mistakes make nothing," I said to him. "You have to forgive yourself just as our committee plans to forgive you. In training, mistakes comes with the territory, but you do need to be a more careful. Stop, Look & Listen, right?" That young man is now one of the finest physicians in his field and has saved countless lives. Yes, I had held him in my morning meditation that day of the scheduled meeting so things worked out as best they could. Having been forgiven with healing kindness, he felt loved throughout a terrible ordeal.

The Way of Listening

Listening is a form of love. Listening takes a lot of humility because otherwise you fill up the room with your own voice, which for some people can be loud and ceaseless. On any given day, I try not to speak as much as I listen, and I reflect back what I have heard to assure another that I take them seriously.

The Way of Carefrontation

There are so many times, every day, when we're called to offer words of encouragement to a friend, loved one, or coworker to help them head in the right direction. Do this with care and great respect. Carefrontation is a thousand times more healing than confrontation because it's full of healing kindness. *Confronting people usually gets you no place.* I keep my letter about carefrontation from M. Scott Peck in a notebook over my office desk.

Concluding Thoughts

Loving-kindness rises above the "thou shalt not" to the "thou shalt." Of course, it is far from enough to get home in the evening and feel good about your day because you did not shout at some innocent wayfarer or worse yet elbow them in the back. That sort of moral minimalism does not take much, at least not for most people. But kindness is more idealistic, more positive, more imaginative. It is not complex and hopefully does not require any training, although good parenting is important early on. Kind people never bully, never harm, never tell people that they have no gifts and talents to develop into full life callings.

CHAPTER 3

The Third Path: May You Follow Your Callings

> "Follow your bliss, and don't be afraid, and doors will open where you didn't know they were going to be."
>
> —Joseph Campbell

Moishe Shagal, later known as Marc Chagall, was born in 1887 in the small Russian Jewish ghetto of Vitebsk, a minor city in what is now Belarus, one of ten children. His father pickled herring; his mother ran a small shop. From the beginning, the odds of Chagall becoming perhaps the greatest painter of the twentieth century were against him.

Chagall's father deplored the idea of his son being an artist and wanted him to pickle herring just like he did. They had a furious father and son argument about this, and in 1908 at age nineteen Marc ran away to St. Petersburg, where he lived and practiced his art. Anti-Semitism was everywhere, and Jews were forbidden to live in St. Petersburg, so he had to avoid the authorities. He lived in small rooms and alleyways, shared cots with other street people, and sold his sketches for a living. Luckily, he was jailed only once on the grounds of his ethnicity.

It was here in St. Petersburg, in the grim conditions Chagall was so willing to tolerate to follow his calling, where the artist had a dramatic spiritual experience that opened a door for him. Chagall's vision would shape his artistic direction and turn his ethereal right-brain world blue for the rest of his life. The essence of Chagall is found in this early experience. He captured it in his autobiography, *My Life,* written some years later in Moscow in 1922:

> My means did not permit me to rent a room; I was forced to content myself with nooks and alcoves. I didn't even have a bed to myself. I had to share it with a workingman. It's true, he was an angel, that workingman with the very black mustache.
>
> He was so kind to me he even flattened himself against the wall to give me more room. Turning my back on him and my face to the window, I breathed fresh air. In those communal recesses, with laborers and pushcart vendors for neighbors, there was nothing for me to do but stretch out on the edge of my bed and think about myself. What else? And dreams overwhelmed me: a bedroom, square, empty. In one corner was a single bed and me on it. It is getting dark. Suddenly, the ceiling opens, and a winged creature descends with great commotion, filling the room with movement and clouds, a swish of wings fluttering. I think: an angel! I can't open my eyes; it's too bright, too luminous. After rummaging about on all sides, he rises and passes through the opening in the ceiling, carrying with him all the light and the blue air. Once again it is dark. I wake up.[59]

Chagall felt guided by this experience to complete *The Apparition*, the subject of which is an angel from his vision. Over the course of his long career, he returned to angels time and time again in his painting and stained-glass windows, usually in the color blue, which for Chagall was the "color of love."

At about this same time, Chagall added the second "l" to his name because in Russian *chagall* means "strode with big steps." Now he was stepping into his calling, and changing his name was part of assuming a new identity that would lead to a future in which he had immense faith despite any adversities.

For the rest of his life, Chagall shaped much of his art around images of blue angels. Thus, he would be unaffected by the artistic movements of his time—cubism, surrealism, and the like—because he was going to capture that interface between the material and nonmaterial where he had experienced his calling. For him, the ethereal was the real. This was where he found his calling, and from this he maintained his spiritual integrity, which meant so much more to him than fame or popularity. He followed his calling as a contrarian.

Most of us find and follow our callings without such an astonishing experience as an apparition, but that was Chagall's path, which was both practical and spiritual. Through it he found inner peace and resilience. For the rest of his life, he painted ethereal images with symbols from every imaginable spiritual tradition, including the Hasidic ones he grew up with. He would often include images of the Cross, as in his famous stained-glass window of the Good Samaritan comprising much of the rear wall of the Union Church in Pocantico Hills, New York. He found his deepest purpose and enjoyed an infinite creative energy that came through him. He did not believe that his images were his own so much as the gifts of a Universal Mind, a flow consciousness that made him feel totally absorbed in his creativity. Famously, and rightly, Pablo Picasso said: "When Chagall paints, you do not know if he is asleep or awake. Somewhere inside his head, there must be an angel."[60]

A Labor of Love

More than just a job or occupation, a calling is a feeling of being beckoned to draw on your abilities. Just as we each have a unique biological fingerprint, we each have a distinctive combination of talents and gifts. In our individual uniqueness, we contribute meaningfully to the lives of others as *a matter of destiny and integrity*.

Callings can be simple or complex, but they are all worthy of equal regard and respect. To have a calling feels so purposeful that many people follow it through thick and thin. With meaning, the sky is the limit. A true calling is a noble purpose for which we feel well-suited and able to express ourselves as free, loving, and creative beings.

Each of us has multiple callings throughout life. They can change, stay the same, or happen simultaneously. For instance, Mahatma Gandhi was simultaneously a spiritual practitioner, social activist, writer, and weaver. Callings can be consuming. It was not easy for Ghandi to be an attentive husband and father at the same time. Finding balance in life is everyone's challenge and finding perfect balance is probably impossible.

Following callings, whether a gradual well-mentored development or a singularly unexpected experience or a combination of these, is not always easy. A calling can feel invasive, breaking into our otherwise routine "good enough" lives and disrupting us to a higher consciousness of who we are meant to be. It often means taking the road less traveled, a road filled with adversity and challenges. But if you love what you are doing and feel called to it for the sake of love, then you will find inner peace. You will never consider straying.

Callings often involve hardships and adversity of all kinds, and you may experience rejection. But following a calling is not about popularity. It requires perseverance. Any so-called "success" in life that contradicts your core values and dreams is not real success and it will leave you running on empty, just going through the external motions. It is easy to be seduced by more money or by working in a prestigious institution that takes you away from your dreams. You may be broke at times, as I was while pursuing my doctorate at the University of Chicago. I could have left and done something more lucrative at the time, which would have been logical since we had a baby on the way, but I took jobs in restaurants around the university, and even sold flowers down in the Loop sometimes. My first teaching job at the University of Detroit-Mercy paid $15,500 per year, but that felt acceptable because I was working with mostly disadvantaged youth who needed a lot of help, and I was teaching them about the Wheel of Love. The feeling of calling was my compensation. Nothing came easy, but we were still at inner peace. Callings require us to keep the light burning bright no matter how strong the wind is blowing.

Callings can bring times of adversity and rejection, but I like to look at life as an artist's expanding canvas. I love Jackson Pollock's art because he began many of his masterpieces by throwing down an unattractive gob of dark paint on the canvas covering the floor of his studio-barn. But he expanded from that point with magnificent colors and lines that seemed to capture the energy of the universe and form a spiritual masterpiece. Callings are not always convenient, but heeding your callings leads to a richer, fuller, more colorful life than would otherwise be the case. In this life there will be many times when we each have to expand the canvas with the energy of Pure Unlimited Love.

There will always be others in your life who insist that they know your callings better than you do, but only you can know your callings. Your callings are your Truth, and no one else's. Others can support you, but they cannot tell you what your callings are. They can also be jealous adversaries who you should view as being there to bring out the best in you. Adversaries are not always the enemies we think they are; often they are blessings. As frustrating as they can be, adversaries unwittingly become your teachers, as you gain insight from them that makes you better at what you do. Overcoming adversity requires sticking with your calling all the more strongly.

Nothing worth doing is ever easy, but it is necessary because callings are what keep you from that dreadful feelings of routinized emptiness. When people don't follow their callings, they don't tap into their gifts fully or even at all. Their highest human potential is lost, and their effervescent energy never engages the world. At work, they feel like the person who waits for Fridays to be liberated. Unable to bring their full self and creativity to their work, these folks feel that an awful lot of their life is wasted. Imagine if their very best energies were readily available for the benefit of others and themselves?

Research on callings is plentiful. An estimated half of working Americans have a sense of meaning and calling in their jobs, which is classic glass half-full. But only about half of those with a sense of calling are able to live this out due to circumstances and lack of opportunity.[61] Those who live out a calling are the happiest workers, the most committed, the least mentally ill, the most engaged, and the most productive. They are also the healthiest. One of my favorite studies shows that older adults who rated high on a purpose of life scale had a 30 percent lower rate of cognitive decline than those who rated low.[62]

Despite the challenges, we follow callings because they take us into the soul zone of love where time stands still. They move us into the flow of creativity and meaning that sometimes feels beyond time and place, as Chagall often felt when immersed in his blue angel painting.

As Shakespeare wrote in *Hamlet*, "To thine own self be true." When you feel called to a vocation or endeavor, you know it. You feel driven, inspired, excited, determined. And you feel ready. Even when things seem to be going poorly and it is hard to make ends meet, you know you are doing what you are meant for. As writer Joseph Campbell, my professor years back when he was visiting the University of Chicago, said, "If you do follow your bliss, you put yourself on a kind of track that has been there all the while, waiting for you, and the life that you ought to be living is the one you are living." Drawing from Campbell's writing, everyone who truly follows their callings is heroic, because the contrary forces of "just fitting in" and maybe making a little more money are strong ones, although people who follow their calling generally do better financially over the long run.

Most people feel called to marriage and procreation, and others don't. But in whatever way, everyone is called to encourage kindness in their kids and to be a good neighbor.

A CALLING AS A MESSAGE FROM THE DIVINE

Historically, the idea of a "calling" was understood as involving the gods. In ancient Greece, people did not believe that creativity came from the human mind alone but from a divine attendant spirit that entered consciousness from some unknowable source that they referred to as "daemons." Even the philosopher Socrates believed that a daemon guided his wisdom and creativity from afar. This may all sound terribly far-fetched to us moderns, but in the twentieth century, the psychiatrist Carl Jung wrote of our being in creative touch with that part of the unconscious mind concerned with higher purpose that "breaks though" into consciousness via inspiring intuitions and dreams.

The Jewish tradition, in a more general sense, describes following a calling using the Hebrew expression **tikkun olam**, or "repairing the world," because it is always possible to do something to help the person in need who is right next to you right now, in some small way.

Whatever the wording, people have often felt pulled toward doing something that employs their unique combination of gifts, allowing them to contribute to the world in one fulfilling way or another. You can feel called to be a writer, a caregiver, an athlete, a baker, a barista, a truck driver, a teacher, an artist, an entrepreneur—anything, really. As you sense that you are using your talents joyfully, meaningfully, and optimally, you are likely on track with your callings.

In an earlier age, one more enchanted than ours, a well-called life was always thought to follow from divine promptings. Everyone, no matter how simple their work, was fulfilling the divine blueprint that gave them a particular set of gifts. But even in modern times, the old language of "gift" remains.

MY RUNAWAY YEAR

It was 1970, and at age seventeen, a starry-eyed teenager (the youthful author himself) felt that he had already awakened to his calling. I had volunteered to teach French-Canadian grade school kids from around Concord, New Hampshire, at the Millville School, just across the road from St. Paul's School, where I was an average student. The Millville kids did not have much money, but they were eager to learn, and I loved tutoring them, as I did on many afternoons. It was fulfilling to see their faces light up when I reassured each of these kids that they had unique talents and really were, as I told them from time to time, "wonders of the universe" and even "miracles of creativity." This made me a better student because I had something to study for that was beyond myself. I learned never to humiliate a student by saying no to their creativity.

Mrs. Marcouse, the principal, encouraged me warmly. She saw how my whole self, mind-heart-body, was bursting with enthusiasm as I bounded up the cement steps into the old red brick schoolhouse. "Mrs. Marcouse, they are each one a special little miracle of creativity," I would tell her. "Any teacher who doesn't see that in them isn't following their right calling."

In July before I was to start college, I got into a massive argument with my parents over a summer job opportunity—tutoring inner city kids in the Bronx. My parents thought the location was too dangerous. "Dad, this is something that I planned on, and it means everything to me," I explained. "It is the one thing I really feel called to do."

"Look, you can't do it. I won't put up with it. That's it. No further discussion." Dad's tone was firm.

I managed a few words of defiance: "This just makes no sense. I feel that this is the job I am destined for."

"You will not take it," my mother said, in a serious, throaty tone.

Dad stood up and commanded with all the strength of the World War II Navy Commander that he had been, "You are upsetting your mother!"

"I am not dropping this job. That's it!" I repeated.

Then, my mom raised the stakes. "I'm paying for Swarthmore College, so either you drop this job or you're on your own."

"Okay, but if I agree with you, I will not be happy. And then what am I supposed to do this summer?"

"I can call Bill," dad said. "Bill has a big lampshade factory. You can make lampshades in Patchogue."

I took the factory job in Patchogue, a little town on the south shore of Long Island. The job lasted for a couple of weeks. Old

Bill, cigar in hand, stationed me on an assembly line cutting cardboard day in and day out. The factory was sweltering. With each passing day, I drove home determined to quit cutting cardboard for good.

One hot, muggy Friday, two weeks into my new job, I drove Dad's aging Mercedes 190 to the factory as usual and put in a solid day's work. That evening, I drove out to Westhampton Beach to spend the weekend with some schoolmates who lived out there. On Saturday, at 11:00 p.m., I got into the 190, said good-bye to my friends without telling anyone about my plans, and started driving west. I followed the Sunrise Highway to the Long Island Expressway. I drove through the Midtown Tunnel, up FDR Drive, over the George Washington Bridge, and then followed the signs for Route 80 West. I did not have a road map, but west is west, and if I couldn't teach in the Bronx, I felt called to go west.

After four hours on Route 80, I began to have real doubts about the propriety of taking Dad's car, although I was feeling angry and dissed about the job. The sun was just starting to rise when I decided to turn around and head home, try to renegotiate things with the folks, and get back to the job I really wanted in the Bronx. If I turned back now, no one would ever know that I was even out on Route 80. At that moment, synchronicity intervened, gracefully but with awesome power.

When I was just about to make a U-turn across the midway so I could head east, the car generator failed and the entire engine went dead, forcing me to coast over to the right shoulder, barely making it to safety. I had all of fifty dollars in my wallet and no credit cards. There I was, stranded in rural Pennsylvania, with only my classical guitar and a small backpack—and nothing but cornfields visible for miles.

So, I did what only an adolescent male with very limited management skills and a typical underdeveloped frontal cortex might do: I took a pencil from the glove compartment and carefully printed in large block letters the following infamous family note on a scrap of paper:

TO THE PENNSYLVANIA STATE POLICE:

Please return this car to Henry A. V. Post, my dad,

        44 Davison Lane East
        West Islip, New York
        Call 516-669-5655.

(From his son Stephen, who no longer works in the lampshade factory!)

As the sun rose, I stood on the side of Route 80 with my thumb out, classical guitar case and backpack at my side, and waited for a ride. The very first vehicle that came along, a big white truck, pulled over and the driver yelled out, "Okay, kid, where you headed?"

"Thanks, sir. Goin' west, looks like!" I told him about how I would never cut cardboard again. The driver, Gary, suggested that I call my mom, but it was too soon. A few days later, I called my mom collect from a phone booth in Nebraska. "Thank God you're alive," she answered, "now we can call off the Pinkertons."

"What, you called the Pinkertons? Detectives! What for? Didn't you get my note?"

"Yup, and dad picked up the car too outside of Lewisburg. We just did not realize how much that teaching job in the Bronx meant to you. *Maybe teaching is your calling after all!*"

"It is that, Mom, a calling. Mom, if a kid finds his calling, he has to stick with it, and you need to respect him for it. He may not have plans, but he has some kind of destiny and feels it."

"Okay. I still don't want you teaching in the Bronx, but if you want to go west, maybe you can sleep on Cousin George's floor for the summer in San Francisco," she suggested. "I can give him a call. And you could call the people at Reed where for some reason they seemed to really want you."

I was seventeen years young but had found myself, and teaching at universities became my life journey for many years. To this day I always bounce up the steps into the medical school with a lot of cheer. I never went to work a single day since to me it was to always play, though I have worked very hard. I was always alive inside, creative, and filled with inner peace. Never for a day was I running on empty, feeling burned out, or just going through the motions. And I never said no to any student with a creative idea that they were passionate about. There is always a way to work that idea even if it has to mature. A "no" without a "yes" is demeaning and can knock well-intentioned students off their callings.

Everyone has a journey worth taking, even if it is just in the formation stage of life. Many stories about following a calling involve adversity, poor communication, and a bit of crazy desperation. But for every person who finds and follows their calling, there is another who has lost sight of theirs. They go through the motions for years and even decades, disenchanted with life and in a state of inner turmoil or resignation.

It is easy to get pulled offtrack. In all these cases, the world loses the best efforts and talents of these individuals—and they grow desperate. But as this desperation deepens and becomes more prevalent, a crisis of societal proportions seems to now be driving many people away from dispiriting endeavors and toward their true callings.

A Crisis of Societal Proportions

For many people, workplace dissatisfaction is high, as reflected in the "Great Resignation" of the early 2020s, during the COVID-19 pandemic, when millions of people—unhappy with pay, hours, commutes, or other conditions—up and quit their jobs, creating an unprecedented labor shortage. This slowdown may have reached an all-time high during the pandemic. According to the Bureau of Labor Statistics, the percentage of people quitting their jobs has been on a steady rise since 2009.[63] Could it be that something is pulling us en masse from emptiness at work toward something better?

People quit jobs because they feel they are squandering their lives. Jodie, for example, had a secure job as an executive secretary at a medical school with a good income and benefits that included a pension. Five years after starting her job at the university, Jodie had a baby and had planned to return to work. During maternity leave, she decided that staying at home with her baby was far more important to her than the income and benefits. At first, her husband objected, but Jodie could not fathom the idea of leaving her baby for what to her had become a meaningless job in comparison.

Even people who are following a calling may reach a point where they are ready to quit because of burnout. Working in healthcare, I am pretty much able to predict who might be quitting soon just from their tone of voice when I ask them if they enjoy their job. It is not that they are responsible for losing the meaning, but rather they are wounded by an environment in which the powers that be destroy meaning. Tired and fed up with a system that forces them to compromise their ideals, these folks stop putting their hearts into service and are just going through the motions, and they lose their sense of calling.

I know a small group of hospital physicians from Cleveland who felt the loss of calling in the modern clinic. But then they went to Peru, and after a few weeks in a refreshing environment doing simple clinical tasks such as clearing earwax out of kids' ears, they came back feeling renewed and created their own primary care clinic where they had more autonomy, could control their schedule, and could take the time to connect with patients again. Managers need to work very seriously at helping employees live into their callings and not beat it out of them in various ways.

Jo-Ann Triner, a friend and the author of *Soulful Work 2.0: Powered by Inner Person Potential*, wants us to imagine the "future of an internally motivated workforce." She once emailed me, "We may wonder why today so many are forsaking jobs that feel too small for their souls? Perhaps we have been trying to squeeze our feet into the steel-toed shoes of our Industrial Age ancestors, whose primitive ways of working we have long outgrown. This quest begins by setting aside the economics-only mindset that has dominated our thinking and left us with a soul deficit that runs too deep for words."[64]

In short, the world needs dreamers.

THE WORLD NEEDS DREAMERS

Dreamers pursue callings over incomes and adversity. They are the people who accomplish the unimaginable—who manage to open doors no one else could—because they follow *their* dreams. The inspirational Black abolitionist Harriet Tubman, born in 1822, escaped slavery and ventured back to the South to lead others to freedom. She was perhaps the most prominent "conductor" on the Underground Railroad, defying danger knowing that were she to be captured, she would be killed. Yet she completed thirteen missions to rescue seventy friends and family members from slavery.

Everyone has hidden talents that, if discovered and honed, dignify the doer and make a maximum impact in our communities. Some of our talents are simple, but all are invaluable. It is possible to find joy in cleaning hospital rooms because there is honor in humbly creating a healing environment for patients. Work done with integrity and excellence always adds dignity to a life. Human dignity is an inherent worth, but there is an added dignity in realizing and developing our callings, however simple or complex.

One of my friends is getting older now but works around our department doing maintenance. She empties the garbage and cleans the bathrooms. She is the most reliable worker around, and she has been at this for years. She is kind to everyone and enjoyable to talk to. She is also tremendously respected. She has a calling. It may not be glamorous, but it is meaningful and of great service to others. When working, she is fully engaged and happy, and she tells me that she prays about her work and the people she serves.

It is only possible to work at the highest level when the inner and outer persons work in tandem. Otherwise, we can be present but only bring half of ourselves to our tasks. We can be dutiful and diligent but not wholehearted and human—we work more like machines than people of substance. We act like professionals but lack the empathy and compassion that characterize a true professional. Detached from this spiritual center, we may feel lost.

"Just Fitting In" Blues

At least part of the solution to this problem is educational because we sometimes educate young people to fit in rather than to find their callings. Author and educator Maria Montessori emphasized individualized instruction and self-paced learning, believing rightly that children are naturally curious and creative. Her greatest book was entitled *To Educate the Human Potential* (1947). We need to encourage young people to discover and trust their callings, for every single young person without exception is a wonder of the universe and a miracle of creativity with a unique set of gifts that destines them to contribute to the lives of others. With any luck, they will also be able to keep a roof over their head and food on the table.

We need an educational culture in which parents and teachers help every young person to discover themselves by serving others meaningfully and flourishing while doing so. Some kids are deeply humiliated and need a lot of love to overcome an unsupportive school environment. Inventor Thomas Edison was once such student who was saved by the love of a great mother.

During my two decades as a professor at Case Western School of Medicine, I would sometimes drive an hour west of Cleveland to visit Edison's birthplace farm in Milan, Ohio, not far from Oberlin. One of the most prolific inventors of the Industrial Age, Edison was expelled from school at age twelve because his teachers had given up on him. They thought he had no focus, no potential, and no hope, and bluntly conveyed this judgment to his mother.

Edison's loving mother encouraged young Thomas to invent things from "junk" items in their big red barn. She told him that someday he might even become "a light to the world," as he did. His mother's love and vision redeemed him from the humiliation he suffered in school. Thomas would spend whole days in their old barn. I used to think about Edison and his mom, who loved him so much that she helped him dream. He was not brilliant in the ways that allowed him to "fit in" at school. He had a different kind of brilliance, an inventiveness that enabled him to see how objects might fit together.

Education today rarely focuses enough on personal vocational identity and meaning. In fact, the system often diverts students from their creative core. There is a bias for uniformity—for all students *fitting into* the same mold and memorizing the same facts. Students can be discouraged from following the inner pull of intrinsic rewards. Later in life, they may find themselves running on empty, lacking intrinsic motivation, and confronting a midlife crisis of meaning or worse.

We need to challenge everyone to discover their creative essence. How can our families and schools help to unveil these unique gifts? How can our educational systems focus on creativity and leadership in all students? Some very creative students may not seem to be the smartest as measured by multiple choice questions or be able to grasp math or science more easily than others. How can teachers ensure that every child is eager to learn, loves attending school, and is creatively engaged? This process involves more than educating children to "succeed" in an eventual job that might leave them running on empty, burned out, and still desperate for meaning.

It is tragic when young people, brimming with potential, are unable to discover their giftedness and flourish because they cannot find encouraging mentors or the resources and environment needed to bring out their infinite potential. We might only discover our gifts when we are nurtured and affirmed by our teachers, role models, and mentors, people who remind us who and what we are. It is upsetting when a person's essential dignity is buried by humiliation, de-dignifying attitudes, and cultures of destruction. Schools, families, spiritual communities, workplaces, neighborhoods, and our culture at large should exist primarily to nurture creative dignity, incrementally with patience and cherishing. Our challenge is to help others reach a fuller awareness and appreciation of who they are and what they can contribute, keeping in mind that all are gifted differently.

We could do more to help students by offering at least two days a week for each to do independent service in their area of giftedness. More could also be done to help students initiate projects, partner with mentors, and carry out projects to meaningful conclusions. Students need the basic knowledge required to function in the workplace and in our democracy. They should likewise be encouraged to follow their callings responsibly and creatively. Without this encouragement, students are in danger of losing their eagerness to learn. They may settle for getting by with passing grades, rewarded only for conforming to the system.

The parental challenge is to raise a child for kindness and for calling. Other forms of success do not matter much in the end. The key is that we feel we are using our gifts in a meaningful way, which generally means that we are being of service to others and not wandering from our path.

Edison's mother, Nancy Elliott Edison, saw his gifts. "Be a light to the world," she told him quoting a biblical passage as he tinkered in the barn. Edison was one of the greatest creative inventors and entrepreneurs of all time and was entirely self-determining. He was in large part inspired by a profound love of all humanity. "The dove is my emblem. I want to serve and advance human life, not destroy it. . . . I am proud of the fact that I have never invented weapons to kill," he stated.[65] Moreover, "I never perfected an invention that I did not think about in terms of the service it might give others. . . . I find out what the world needs, then I proceed to invent."[66]

In his adult heyday as the "wizard" of Menlo Park in New Jersey, Edison affirmed his love of work. "Personally, I enjoy working about 18 hours a day. Besides the short catnaps I take each day, I average about four to five hours of sleep per night." How did this man, who only had three months of formal schooling as a child before his teacher determined that he was "brain scrambled" and did not belong in school, who had to be home taught, who at age fourteen became totally deaf in his left ear and 80 percent deaf in his right, and who would for a while be a young beggar on the streets of New York, define his creativity? "Genius," he stated, "is one percent inspiration, ninety-nine percent perspiration."[67]

Edison's true purpose to enhance humankind allowed him to endure failure after failure, including the more than 10,000 failed attempts to find a filament for an electric light bulb. He's often quoted as saying, "If I find 10,000 ways something won't work, I haven't failed. I've just found 10,000 ways that won't work."[68] The outcome of his efforts included the light bulb, the electric motor, the phonograph, the alkaline battery, and countless other devices that we all take for granted today. This middle-school dropout netted 1,368 patents in all.

Working from Our Hearts

Imagine if our educational systems could focus on the student discerning their calling, enabling them to pursue wondrously productive lives, and look back in old age with gratification for a life lived well. Imagine if we could link education to service and volunteerism in ways that students find meaningful and are then able to carry this meaning into their occupations, careers, and professions. The inner peace and productivity of our lives and society would be greatly expanded. Immense human potential would be unlocked—not because we are any smarter but because we are profoundly purpose driven. We would also be healers of the world, regardless of our occupation.

Imagine if schools allowed people of every spiritual tradition to meditate on such things as the universal Golden Rule. I am not talking about praying in school. Students could practice meditation at the start of the class day on themes such as loving-kindness and healing purposes. Grade schools like Coleman Elementary School in Baltimore have been doing something unusual when students misbehave. Rather than punishing children and sending them to the principal's office, they send them to the Mindful Moment Room instead. This room is filled with nice decorations and purple pillows. It has windows galore. The kids are encouraged to sit down and go through breathing and meditation practices, and they are invited to talk about what happened in a calm manner. This allows them to avoid destructive emotions, and also seems to help their attention spans and concentration so they learn better over the course of the day. They have a "holistic" program that goes well beyond something just for those who may misbehave. It encompasses the entire school and offers an afterschool program. During school hours, everyone pauses for a "mindful moment." The coordinator says that while we might not think that kids would meditate in silence, they do. In *Oprah Magazine* (August 2016) the parents claimed that their kids came home less stressed out and even encouraged their parents to breathe and meditate. The Mindful Moment program is sponsored by the Holistic Life Foundation in more than 185 schools, with everyone happily involved (see https://holisticlifefoundation.org for more details and information). Students are more focused, calmer, eager to learn, and peaceful in their interactions.

Many of the behavioral problems in our grade schools and high schools might diminish if this practice occurred daily across the country. It might be followed by a fifteen-minute small group reflections circle, where any child could speak from the heart about gratitude, kindness, honesty, purpose, forgiveness, and hope for the day—or about something with which they are struggling in their lives. Such inner-person exercises help children learn rules of gentle kindness: respond, never react to what is being said; a thoughtful question is usually much better than an answer; be affirming and never judgmental. Kids can build circles of trust and form identities of kindness that displace more critical and exclusive behaviors. They will go on to build meaningful dreams for their futures and have real reasons to learn. This is intrinsic motivation at its best.

Such habits of the heart can be nurtured all the way from grade school to high school and beyond, resulting in healthier, happier, and more fulfilled students who will almost certainly find their callings.

Of course, even if this is happening in schools, it may not be happening in the home. Parents and schools need to be on the same creative page, and that is not always the case, as evidenced by the boy who ended up with dad's car stuck on some Pennsylvania highway. But it is a step in the right direction.

We offer mindfulness experiences in medical schools on an elective basis, and I offer a course, cotaught with some of our very best medical students and faculty, called "The Compassionate Care Toolkit," which meets for three hours two days per week for four weeks in the final fourth year. It always enrolls the maximum fifteen students, and many go on to do research on the topics. They seem to have found a special calling and go on to teach their own courses at various medical centers.

Knowing That You Have Found It

I believe that my job is to help students find that steady flow state, where their immersion in a task involves the whole self. When students are so engaged that they lose sense of time, then and only then am I a good professor.

If you are stuck struggling to find a calling, ask yourself not what you want to be but *what problems you want to solve and who you feel called to serve. Your calling does not have to be grand or spectacular externally. It only has to connect with the heart.* What matters is that you are doing what you love. In the end, following a calling is following the way of love.

Since we live in an age of possessive individualism and materialism, it is even more important to talk about high purpose and calling. To suggest that every human being is a unique wonder of the universe can be a hard sell, but it is true. We are each totally unique, and a simple job is fine if we do it well and with meaning. Whatever gifts and talents you have, use them to serve the world, and then you have fulfilled your calling. This is what you are on this earth to do.

It is a good idea to keep a journal and write down your perspectives on the experience of feeling called. Meditation is helpful to keep the depth of a calling in consciousness and memory. These internal exercises can keep you from getting confused. You may not know if your work is really a calling. Often in our contemporary culture we think of a calling in terms of individualism and selfishness. People speak about "callings" in possessive individualistic ways and the accumulation of greater and greater wealth. In this case, you may have a job but not a calling.

Maybe you don't ever have to find your calling, but if you are willing to serve others in kind giving, your calling will find you. This book starts with chapters entitled "May You Give and Glow" and "May You Heal with Kindness" because when you begin to abide in these paths, *you naturally fall into callings* that draw on your gifts. You never want to be running to catch an opportunity that is not your purpose. Living a life of callings is to be purposeful, or filled with nobility of service and kindness.

Tips for Finding and Following Your Callings

- Spend time around people who seem to be willing to experiment with their gifts. Many people do this naturally. Aristotle wrote a lot about friendship. True friends, he argued, are the ones who recognize your gifts and help you pursue them. Gather together with like-minded friends so you can debrief about your journey.
- Spend time alone in nature and reflect quietly about what you might need to do to develop your calling more fully. Who might you go visit? Is there a school you want to go to? With persistence, you can find support.
- Once you start following your callings, cultivate an attitude of gratitude. Remember that you are fortunate to be on the right pathway. Breathe a sigh of relief because maybe just a few months ago you felt lost. Keep a notebook of the things you are most grateful for when it comes to following your calling, and how it makes you feel deep down to have landed on it.
- Reflect with your friends on how contributing to the lives of others is unfolding in your life and how you are thinking today about the purpose of your life in new ways.
- Roll up your sleeves. There is no substitute for making the effort, both for your own success and for your community.
- Ask yourself: Am I treating people with kindness? Am I a good listener, a good helper, uplifting others, the kind of person everyone likes to have around? Is kindness a daily goal? Can others count on me to be diligent?

- Reconsider your calling, if need be. If not fulfilled, ask yourself: Am I enjoying my work? Blurring the line between work and play? Being cheerful? Feeling fulfilled? If not, maybe reconsider your calling.
- Stick with your calling, even when tempted to stray by money or prestige. Believe in the beauty of your calling.
- Meditate about your calling at work. Take a few minutes at least once a day, especially at the end of the day, and be mindful of how you feel, of how stressed out you might feel, of whether you are running on empty and not taking time to connect with your colleagues.
- Try to build community and mutual support. Help other people find their callings and be a good role model for them. Pass the torch of meaning and purpose to others. Be a mentor to everyone.
- Volunteer (see sidebar below).

EXPERIMENT

Many people, whatever their age, find their true calling in life by experimenting. As a national expert on volunteering and health, my recommendation for those who struggle to find their calling or who feel empty at work and want something more meaningful is to volunteer. Why, exactly?

1. There is transformative power in volunteering. When we help others, we have reasons to learn and work that go beyond self and reach others. The self on its own is simply not as exciting as the self in service.
2. We can develop the capacity to find meaning in serving others and nurturing the community.
3. We can discover our skills and then develop them. We can move from volunteering to becoming full-fledged professionals.

4. Volunteering can be a catalyst for self-confidence and personal empowerment, as well as the development of leadership skills we might find useful in a calling.
5. Volunteering gives some people an opportunity for international experience. Volunteer travel is a great path to self-discovery.
6. Volunteering can enhance resilience and replenishment. I have worked with students who were feeling burned out, but by taking a few weeks in the summer to provide free medical care in Peru, they were refreshed. Volunteering allowed them to reconnect with the kind of meaning that brought them into medicine in the first place.
7. Volunteering helps people learn that in the search for their calling, it can be very helpful to step out of one's comfort zone and try something they could never have imagined themselves doing.

My Morning Meditation

I have been an unusually successful mentor in medical schools. I have two rules: Never say no without a yes, and always be available, affable, and able. There is no creative idea that cannot be developed and worked with, and being fully present rather than distracted makes all the difference.

One day, a student from Brooklyn came to my office door to announce that she was leaving medical school after two years. She came from abject poverty, her mom was a housekeeper, she never met her dad, and she didn't feel she fit in with her peers. Yet she was a brilliant student in college, and Stony Brook University is highly ranked for upward mobility in such young people. I had a packed schedule that afternoon, but I dropped everything and spent the next three hours listening to her. I encouraged her to take a year off and do reflective writing under my mentorship, which she did. My wife and I drove into Brooklyn monthly to take her to a restaurant that she liked. Her essays improved as she gained clarity around her thought process, and she returned to school the next year. Now she practices medicine and has a wonderful little family.

In the early mornings I would meditate and visualize this student, and sometimes say, as the Japanese Buddhists do, "I honor the divine in you." And I would ask myself what I can offer her on our next visit. Usually, I would get some intuitive insight that I was otherwise missing. Essentially, I was meditating and praying for her to find her calling—and to not to give up.

The Wheel of Love in the Pursuit of Callings

The Way of Celebration

When someone is seeking or following their callings, we can rejoice with them. Love means rejoicing in the presence of another, in that person's existence, and in his or her achievements. They have stepped forward into their meaningful destiny, and therefore we must rejoice. This is no small thing. Have a "callings" dinner at home or a restaurant and show your gratitude.

The Way of Compassion

People suffer deeply when they have not been able to blur the line between work and play and they are just going through the motions but never really engaging their true callings and creative capacities. I never get upset with a med school colleague who seems to no longer "hear the music" of healing in the way that they did when they first broke into healthcare. Every year, doctors and nurses commit suicide because they can no longer put their heart into their work, and they grow depressed. Depression often follows from that loss of calling. So, we need to be kind, empathic, and compassionate in helping others find their way back to a sense of calling. Those with no callings are suffering, and we must respond actively and compassionately to reduce that suffering.

The Way of Helping

If we are honest, there are always helpers along the journey as we find and follow our callings. Be grateful to those people, whether mentors, teachers, role models, or encouragers. And pass the torch forward by helping others find themselves. We can keep a list of the major mentors who have helped us along the path or who we have helped and include them in our morning meditations.

The Way of Forgiveness

Following a calling is often a story of experimentation and forgiveness. When I finally did get back to West Islip, I thanked my dad for going out to Pennsylvania to pick up that broken-down old Mercedes 190. And I apologized because my auto heist was a little extreme. I acknowledged that while I was angry, there might have been a better way to handle things, yet I stayed firm in my resolve not to go back to the lampshade factory. Anyway, the details are forgotten with the passage of time. Help others by letting grudges fade.

The Way of Listening

Anyone seeking their callings has to be ready to listen to them—to the hints and whispers saying, "Hey, this is something you can try." It might even be that you have a dream about yourself doing something that you find a bit surprising. In helping others find their callings, we have to turn off our usual talkativeness and enter into a kind of attentiveness to the other that is unconditional. We must meet people where they are, as they are, and allow them to find comfort in our simply being there.

The Way of "Carefrontation"

When following callings, you want to experience "carefrontation." You want to have friends who caringly confront you when maybe you're about to give up and get stuck forever. And you want to be able to kindly let people you love know that they are veering offtrack and need to have a little more faith in their destiny and their gifts. One key expression of love is the readiness to remain graceful and caring while confronting someone who needs to stay on course.

The Way of Loyalty

Most of us live two lives—one that we learn from and one that is better as a result of having learned. When loyal to our callings, we are loyal and true to ourselves, and we grow through these endeavors. Constancy offers the possibility of deepening a calling over time. Every now and then, we might be on the brink of quitting when something happens to keep us loyal to our calling—an unforeseen opportunity or a chance meeting. Still, some callings may end at some point. Sometimes a calling is completed, and we are loyal to our deeper selves when we move on.

The Way of Respect

We have to respect someone's choice to follow a calling, even if it is not the calling we anticipated. Chagall's father was probably an excellent herring pickler, but it was disrespectful to think his son Marc was going to be a happy pickler. Minimally, respect implies an unwillingness to manipulate or overpower someone as they pursue meaningful aspiration. Respect does not seek to absorb the other into the self; it recognizes and accepts the "other as other," while retaining an intense interest in them and their well-being. In this sense, love keeps its distance even as it draws near and manifests a certain hesitation as it holds the callings of others as inviolable.

A great deal of human cruelty stems directly from an irreverent unwillingness to respect the lives, thoughts, and feelings of others.

The Way of Mirth

Never rebuke the merry child-eyed starry wanderer who is seeking their callings. I knew a wonderful preacher who carried two books everywhere he went: the Gospels and a collection of tasteful jokes for all occasions. When you are helping someone with their search, and even challenging them a bit, don't get so solemn that you forget the beauty of laughter.

Bob Hope lived to be one hundred, dying on July 27, 2003. What made him so great? His mirth and laughter brought smiles to millions via movies, television, and the stage. Beginning with World War II, over the course of fifty years, Hope entertained troops serving in six different wars. He had clearly found his calling by lovingly delivering tasteful humor to people who could use a laugh.

When you move forward in callings, levity is one way to express love. It is hard to imagine loving someone with whom you can't laugh, at least a little.

The Way of Creativity

To find and follow callings, we have to stay in touch with our creativity, even when things get tough. For instance, Bonnie was diagnosed with multiple myeloma. On her first visit to the hospital, she was taken into a treatment room and given a small, gray blanket to put on her lap. Bonnie thought this was sad. "When I got home," she told me, "I started knitting, a pastime that I had always found calming. It didn't take long before I had a pretty, colorful lap blanket. I made a few and then it came to me—I could bring these into the oncology department for other patients to use during their treatment."

"What started as a little project," Bonnie continued, "has become my full-time job. I make about two blankets per day and when I have about fifteen, I take them to the hospital. Each blanket has a tag that says "Free—To keep you warm during treatment." Each person can keep the blanket and take it home. The receptionist told me that within a half-hour all the blankets are gone. At my request, the patients never know where their present has come from. Since I started making the blankets, my blood tests have improved. My oncologist said, 'I have no way to explain this medically. All I can say is, just keep making blankets.' Nothing in my life has given me more joy or personal satisfaction except the birthing of my three sons." Bonnie has found a calling. She expresses love through creativity.

Concluding Thoughts

In so many ways, a calling is the expression of the human desire to Give and Glow and to heal this world, and thus it comes third in our set of Seven Paths to inner peace and flourishing. Callings allow us to develop and sustain these peaceful strengths over the course of our lifetimes.

It is my belief that American youth are entering an era of unsurpassed creativity, despite cultural and educational challenges. Perhaps I am biased, but after four decades of teaching medical students, they seem to be more creative and kinder than ever. We are all called to do the work of loving. Love "calls us out." So many of these students are fabulous models of dignity in pure love. They stand out because they are dreamers and they believe in the beauty of their dreams.

CHAPTER 4

The Fourth Path: May You Raise Kind Children

> "You give but little when you give of your possessions. It is when you give of yourself that you truly give."
>
> —Kahlil Gibran

In the early 2000s, shortly after cofounding the Institute for Research on Unlimited Love and while still a professor in Cleveland, I received a call from an adolescent psychiatry institution. A young woman had tried to kill herself. She told the hospital psychiatrists that she did not want to live anymore because human nature is so brutal and nasty. She wondered, *what then is the point of life?*

This young woman had spent a few days in the hospital under twenty-four-hour observation before the psychiatrists eventually called and asked whether I would talk with her. They felt they weren't making much progress. At the time, I was supporting researchers around the country who were studying human nature and kindness. I accepted the invitation.

I went to the hospital and into this young person's room after observing the security guard stationed at the door to prevent any further suicide attempts. What first caught my eye was their shelf—*Being and Nothingness* (1943) by Jean Paul Sartre, *The Lord of the Flies* (1954) by William Golding, and *The Selfish Gene* (1976) by Richard Dawkins—all classics. For Sartre if anyone looks at you with kindness, watch out because they are ultimately manipulative. Golding, following Sigmund Freud, explores the dark side of human nature, and Dawkins tells us that even if we might be deluded into thinking that we are kind, we are at a deeper level just the unwitting conduits for "selfish" genes to replicate themselves into future generations. In high school, we all read Robert Ardrey's *The Territorial Imperative*, a very nasty image of non-human primates. Such books sent negative messages about the nature of humankind, including that kids are born selfish and that under the most circumstances, our inherently brutal natures will surface. This young woman was just drinking in the unscientific assumptions of the twentieth century with their dark philosophy of human nature. She could have benefitted from some better science and philosophy, and that was what the Institute was all about. Some years later Jane Goodall would offer the culture much better studies about the often very kind and even compassionate behavior of apes in nature.

Current messaging is shifting, with plays and movies appealing to children—such as *Maleficent* and *Wicked*—exploring how circumstances turn naturally kind beings into villains. But for the most part, twentieth-century literature, science, and philosophy were badly mistaken about the nature of the toddler and young child, indicating that kids are born nasty and selfish, like little seething cauldrons of vile ego controlled only by the thin veneer of civilization. In this psychiatric ward, I saw how these works by major twentieth-century figures sent the message to an otherwise kind kid that their *kindness is fake news, not real.* No wonder this kid was feeling down about the world. She had been slowly taught to give up on being a good human being.

We've learned a lot about kindness since Sartre, Golding, and Dawkins first wrote their texts. Since 2000, more than fifty excellent scientific investigations have indicated that the very young child, the toddler, is by nature empathic. Some of the best studies have come from psychologist Paul Bloom of the Yale Child Studies Center, but there are many others from around the world. The most current research has shown that those who described the child as entirely nasty and egocentric were in error. Thanks to new and better science, the twentieth-century cynicism about the nature of the child has given way to a kinder image.

We've learned that kindness is there partly by nature, but the right supportive buttons do need to be pushed. *Kindness depends on the quality of a child's exchange with their surrounding world, and that exchange occurs in their families long before a child speaks any words.* Kindness in the child can only be awakened by kindness, and so it's become more and more evident that we must raise kind children—or leave them without hope in a world in which it becomes more and more difficult to navigate.

THE CHILD: KIND BY NATURE *AND* NURTURE

Science today says that children are born to be kind. Bloom observes babies and toddlers. In a study, hundreds of them independently watched three puppets. Puppet One tries to climb up an incline but falls down. Puppet Two helps by pushing them up to the top. Puppet Three pushes Puppet One down. After watching the skit several times, the toddlers showed a preference for Puppet Two, as evidenced by gaze and touch. They identified with and rooted for kindness. "It wasn't just a statistical trend; just about all babies reached for the good guy."[69]

But it is not quite so simple. The Yale studies also reveal a disturbing aspect of human nature that is clear before age one: A child who prefers Cheerios over graham crackers for a snack will slam a lid down on the helper puppet's head 87 percent of the time if the helper chooses graham crackers. There seems an innate tendency to create an "us" versus "them" category and to maltreat "them."[70]

Various experiments show how easy it is to fan children's favoritism into aggression, especially using a negative reward system, such as when bullies gain popularity among their peers. One out of three students worldwide report being bullied. People who have been hurt will hurt others. Despite antibullying laws and prevention programs, two-thirds of bullies continue their bad behavior and three-quarters of bullied kids are still bullied. Research indicates that bullied kids do less well academically and are at risk for mental and physical suffering. A Secret Service study showed that 71 percent of school shooters have been bullied.[71] By age three or four, Protestant children in Belfast hate Catholics, and vice versa; the same can be said for children in many other places.[72] In-group/out-group tensions are clear from very early on in a child's development—whether regarding race, religion, class, ethnicity, intelligence, pedigree, or appearance.

Some children may be more genetically wired for kindness than others, but all children can still learn to be kind if they are raised in a healthy family and culture. It is possible to nurture kindness in children. An old Buddhist parable that goes something like this tells us how:

"A fight is going on inside me between two wolves. One is bad. It is cruelty, anger, resentment, arrogance, and selfishness. The other is good. It is kindness, peace, forgiveness, humility, and generosity. The same fight goes on inside us all."

"Which one will win, Grandmother?"

"The one you feed."[73]

WHAT CHILDHOOD KINDNESS LOOKS LIKE

Sean Keener, who as much as any researcher delves into the child's experience of love (which is often expressed through kindness), asked a group of kids, "What does love mean?" The answers were surprisingly deep:[74]

"When my grandmother got arthritic, she couldn't bend over and paint her toenails anymore. So, my grandfather does it for her all the time, even when his hands got arthritis too. That's love."—Rebecca, age 8

"When someone loves you, the way they say your name is different. You just know that your name is safe in their mouth."—Billy, age 4

"Love is what's in the room with you at Christmas if you stop opening presents and listen."—Bobby, age 7

A six-year-old child saw an old man crying, having lost his wife of many years. The boy went into the old man's yard and sat down next to him. His mother asked him what he said to their neighbor. The boy answered, "Nothing, I just helped him cry."—Jimmy, age 6

THE PROBLEM WITH UNKINDNESS

Growing up in an unkind or hostile environment has consequences. Parents often fail to understand the lasting effects of what are known as Adverse Childhood Experiences (ACEs), which have been found to be a major factor in future unkindness and poor mental and physical health. I have investigated ACEs in the context of adolescent addiction, where it is often a contributing cause. Although many studies show that these early life detriments can be overcome in adolescence and adulthood with good communities and relationships, various types of abuse, neglect, and trauma are known to reduce well-being later in life.

A 1998 study examined more than 17,000 people who received a medical evaluation and completed surveys about their childhood experiences, current health status, and behaviors. ACEs were found to have an unequivocal impact on public health. More than half of the individuals who responded to the survey reported at least one early traumatic experience. More trauma corresponded with greater risks of destructive behavior and illicit substance use, psychological issues, and reduced life expectancy.[75]

The same relationship was found between the number of ACEs reported on the survey and the number of negative health outcomes experienced in later life, including heart disease, cancer, and skeletal fractures. Some of the more salient outcomes and risk behaviors included depression, suicide attempts, alcoholism, and drug use.[76] It seems that if we could place more emphasis on raising kind children, this would lighten up the load on some doctors and nurses.

Children who aren't nurtured from infancy and beyond with tender loving care have what I call "love deficit disorder." These kids are more likely to suffer some adverse consequences. Our goal in rearing children should be the generative production of love energy on the earth as it adds to the inner peace of both parents and kids. No child, no family, and no society can flourish without love. Indeed, the very life and death of humankind depends on this one great energy. It is mainly produced by small groups, such as the family, during the early years of life. Kind parents produce creative figures of love who do good in the world. We can reduce the number of individuals who do harm if we create loving homes.

It is much easier to nurture a child through wise love than it is to transform a selfish adult into a generous person with a kind heart. Sudden or gradual transformations happen but are usually difficult for an individual who regards early life as an obstacle to overcome rather than as a time of growth.

In contrast to ACE children, kids raised in kindness are healthier mentally and physically in adulthood. Researchers examined data gathered from two groups of adolescents first interviewed in California in the 1930s and subsequently interviewed every ten years until the late 1990s. They looked at what's known as generativity, or behavior that indicates intense positive emotion extending to all humanity. The results of the study showed that adolescents who want to give or do give kindly become, in general and to varying degrees, psychologically and physically healthier adults.[77]

Kids are generally kind and compassionate by nature, but this wonderful inclination can be overwhelmed by ACEs and if parents push the wrong buttons by role modeling destructive emotions. It is said widely that "hurt people hurt people." Both aggression and kindness begin in the family, and the healthier the family unit, the greater the chance of raising kind and flourishing children.

THE IMPORTANCE OF WISE PARENTAL LOVE

It takes a village to raise children well, and we can all contribute, but there is a certain obvious primacy to the parent-child relationship that must be honored. When it comes to all the effort, energy, and investment that goes into childrearing, four parental hands are for the most part better than two. *The nuclear family is an indispensable asset because it ideally provides a child with loyal and committed primary caregivers, dedicated lifelong parental love, and a fitting education in spiritual and moral values, etiquette, and support.* In general, when it comes to raising kind children, which I consider the primary reason for marriage in addition to married benevolent love, four loving hands are indeed better than two. Unloving hands, harsh and unkind, benefit no child.

Pitirim Alexandrovich Sorokin, Harvard's first professor of sociology, studied "good neighbors" in the United States dating back to the 1950s. He looked at large numbers of people who were identified by their peers as generous, kind, and helpful. When asked to identify the factors that contributed to their being good neighbors, 21 percent indicated religion, 29 percent parental and family training, 8 percent education and schooling, 11 percent personal experience, and 28 percent universal life experience; less than 1 percent mentioned books. He concluded that family and parents are the most important factors in the "altruization" of humanity, followed by general life experience (minus family and religion), and religion. The role of educational institutions is modest.[78] The child is primarily formed and raised by good parents, and while others can be good helpers and role models, good parents are the key.

The Greeks have a special word, *storge*, for parental love because of its warmth, depth, and commitment. All great thinkers have recognized the central role of the stable family in raising children. John Stuart Mill in *Utilitarianism* devoted the last quarter of his book to the natural affections and warmth of the family. He saw the family as the indispensable centerpiece of "the greatest happiness of the greatest number," for without the family we would suffer in misery and want. Families that devote themselves to raising kind children without being overindulging or ineffective experience *storge*.

But love and kindness extend beyond family. When children learn that only people within their narrow kin lineage are worth consideration and care, love stops short. Philosopher and revolutionary socialist Karl Marx saw the biological family as an obstacle to the fair distribution of property across society, especially adversely impacting those born into economic hardship. Other philosophers have concocted "utopian" schemes for an ideal society, in which children are raised by the State, as in Plato's *Republic*. Plato felt that the family was counterproductive, emphasizing its faults, including its tendency to concentrate wealth in a narrow band and limiting the potential for upward mobility among the lower economic classes. Aristotle later corrected Plato by arguing that without the biological bond of the parent-child axis, it is hard to imagine how kindness would be successfully passed on to children, for it is taught primarily by role models who are intentional about it.

My hope in this chapter is to make raising kind children the absolute core aspiration behind bringing children into the world. Aldous Huxley's *Brave New World* places a world without families in the category of dystopia—that is, referring to the worst society possible. Mothers and fathers do not even exist in such a world: There is no memory of them, and therefore no effort is made to raise children to be kind.

This Platonic denial of all family values underlies the introduction of neologisms that do away with the words "mother" and "father" in favor of expressions such as "a birthing progenitor." The most radical antifamily ideologues would replace the words "mother" and "father" with Parent 1 and Parent 2. This is not a direction we should take. Evolutionarily, the functional family is where kindness and compassion and other character strengths are passed down and role modeled. Abolishing or sterilizing the parent-child relationship with such cold terms is not promising.

Mothers and fathers each have distinct roles in relation to a son or a daughter. There is lots of evidence indicating that fatherless male adolescents lack their essential role model, and many (certainly not all) suffer from this in the form of higher criminal behavior, psychological problems, educational failure, and moral debilitation. Moreover, children *in general* get better material support, parental involvement, and role modeling of kindness in a home where the father is present. The report "Beyond Rhetoric: A New American Agenda for Children and Families" stated that "rising rates of divorce, out-of-wedlock childbearing, and absent parents are not just manifestations of alternative lifestyles, they are patterns of behavior that increase children's risks of negative consequences."[79]

AN ANCIENT AND RESPECTED PRACTICE

Some of the parents who are most thoughtful about raising kind kids are those who for various reasons cannot reproduce. Sometimes they can find help in fertility clinics and with in vitro fertilization, or surrogacy. But this does not always work. When it doesn't, they can fall back on the ancient and respected practice of adoption established in the very earliest codes of law going back to that of Hammurabi (Stone 7), the first king of the Babylonian Empire (present-day Iran) nearly four thousand years ago. It has long survived as the most successful and ubiquitous solution worldwide to raising children whose biological parents for one reason or another wish to freely relinquish them or who have passed away. A good definition of "adoption" by two adoptive parents I know is this: "the act of taking a child into your home and heart by choice." They had to overcome so many obstacles, legal and otherwise, that by the time they succeeded, there was no doubt in anyone's mind that they would be very responsible and caring parents.

John Eastburn Boswell, the great historian of the family and the ways of family formation in the West through the Renaissance, sums up the practice of adoption as follows: "Society relied on the kindness of strangers to protect its extra children, a kindness much admired and prominent in the public consciousness."[80] Europe, he shows, relied on "a panoply of formal and informal arrangements" for providing a family for children in need.[81]

In Christian ethics, all believers are, as St. Paul stressed, "adopted" into Christ. At the deepest level, no one possesses a child or another human being. God alone possesses. Even biological parents are nothing more and, importantly, nothing less than caring stewards with the primary task of being good role models for loving-kindness.

Developmental psychologist Mary Ainsworth of Johns Hopkins University found that the kind of mother a baby has predicts emotional traits later in life. She observed interactions between mothers and infants and divided the mothering styles into three categories. A year later, she tested the emotional qualities of the toddlers by observing their responses to brief separations. Mothers who had been warm, tender, and consistently responsive raised a "secure" toddler who used their mother as a haven from which to explore the environment. Such a toddler became fussy and upset when the mother left the room but reached out to her with smiles when she returned. They were easy to console when their mothers picked them up. These toddlers were *secure*.

A cold, resentful mother produced an *insecure-avoidant* toddler who was indifferent to their mother's departures and ignored her return, focusing instead on items such as a toy in a corner. Another group was clingy, refused to explore the room independently, and became anxious and agitated when their mothers left the room. They also cried frequently. The toddlers reached out when the mothers returned but arched away and resisted the mother's attempts to console them. These toddlers had experienced inconsistent and erratic emotional interactions during their first year of life. Ainsworth called them *insecure-ambivalent* toddlers.

What happened to these toddlers as they grew older? The securely attached toddlers developed into empathic, caring, happy, resilient, likable grade-schoolers who had friends and tended to seek out help when needed. Infants who had cold mothers became distant, hostile to authority, and difficult-to-reach grade-schoolers. They would not ask for comfort even if hurt, and they tended to provoke and upset other kids. Those who had been frustrated in infancy and childhood became aggressive and hurtful adolescents. The infants of inconsistent and erratic mothers were timid, lacking in confidence, and easily frustrated. They asked for help even when they could do things for themselves. The insecurely attached were susceptible in adolescence to delinquency, substance abuse, pregnancy, and other problems. They were also less popular.

The dynamic between a mother and an infant matters a lot. Tender loving care leads to emotional health and fosters empathy and caring. The key is for the infant to experience consistent, empathic, soothing interactions with the caregiver. It is also important that the caregiver's facial expressions mirror the baby's sadness or joy, thereby creating comfort and trust. Babies who do not experience any response, or who receive harsh and hostile responses, become fearful and distrustful. The experience of joyful empathy helps the infant to develop a whole emotional soul, complete with more neuronal synapses than would develop in those who live in isolation and fear.[82]

THE SPIRITUALITY OF PROCREATION

Let me be perfectly clear: not everyone wants to marry and have kids, nor should they. And there are countless ways to help raise kind kids in so many social roles other than biological parenthood, although this does have a certain natural primacy.

Yet many people view marriage and procreation as a natural duty, or even more mystically, as was the case before modern times. I like the word "procreation," which is a more mystical and much older word than the modern "reproduction," which is only as old as Henry Ford's manufacturing plants in Detroit. "Procreation" is beautiful, like the word "re-creation" (to "re-create"), in that centuries ago it referred to the wonderful ways in which face-to-face play constantly refreshes our hearts and minds.

In some traditions, the Mind underlying the universe is manifest in the procreative union that brings forth new life, and these traditions surround marriage and childbirth with innumerable rituals, prayers, meditations, and sacred texts. In the dyadic creative communion of male and female, we see the image of "God," the universal creative energy. The Hebrew scripture sums up the purpose of creation for most people with the phrase "Be fruitful and multiply."[83]

Across nature, procreation is something of a divine ordinance without which life ends and species pass away. Most images of divine nature, whether East and West or North and South, include a dualism of masculine and feminine elements, mother and father. They hold that these two attributes exist within the deity and hence are exhibited throughout the universe. Wherever we turn our eyes, we behold these two principles. Spiritual people in almost every tradition have intuited that nature at its best is a signpost to the divine. From the Platonic perspective, the natural world results from divine craftsmanship, and nature is a means of discovering divine patterns.

Such metaphysics confer upon marriage a sacred status and the ideal of permanence. We join with the divine in creation as procreative beings, though this is not quite uniform as some people are born and destined for singleness or other gender specificities. Without a spiritual foundation, marriage is easily trivialized with the overvaluation of passionate infatuation that is always fleeting and never as substantial as spiritual companionship. In affirming this, there should be no gendered tradition of domination. On the contrary, authentic marriage requires the flow of love between two beings of equal worth and dignity mutually recognized and acknowledged.

Love in the Home: A Spiritual Foundation for a Kind Marriage

Creating a family culture of love in which children can flourish and become kind requires that adults in the household have a mostly peaceful relationship. *Hurt people hurt people.* High conflict marriages have negative lasting effects, especially when children are "weaponized" by their parents as each tries to enlist the child's support for their side of the fight. Marriages in which parents argue a lot are painful for children.

Raising a kind child starts with both parents focusing their minds on achieving a culture of kindness in their marriage relationship.[84] Parents need to believe that raising a kind child is the most important responsibility they have. When a couple really works at the art of empathic, nonviolent, and respectful communication, this spills over into their children's lives. When parents are in conflict, children absorb this and imitate the language and behavior. Parents should decide before they have children that they will not have heated arguments in their child's presence and serve instead as kindness role models. Repetitive trauma witnessed by children is a constant stressor that inhibits their innate kindness.

Parents who are divorced or separated can always commit to modeling kindness to one another though respectful communication and language, especially in the presence of their children whatever the arrangements affirmed by the courts. We have to give grace and equal care to the estimated 50 percent of families in which parents are divorced, and yet they still can and do firmly commit to raising kind children by treating each other respectfully and implementing family rules in both homes. When we look upon our children and observe them living kind lives and doing kind things in the world, all the challenges of rearing children feel infinitely worthwhile.

How can parents avoid or resolve the problem of conflict? It is never avoided entirely. This is where spiritual practice is essential. Mindfulness practices can help with emotional self-control, meditation can focus the emotions on inner peace, and an awesome experience in nature can be soothing. For those who are prayerful, this can help along with an emotionally healthy religious community. A lasting kind marriage that nurtures kindness between partners and in children gains support from a spiritual worldview in this most important and potentially life-creating relationship.

Kindness between spouses is passed down like a sacred torch to children. Children notice all the details of parental interactions, and if they see and hear mostly simmering hostility and harsh arguments, they are left feeling sad and unloved. Coldness covers their small universe and stiffens the flow of love, and if this is protracted, the results can be damaging long term. If we want to raise caring children, we as couples need to care for one another, even in the context of divorce. A relationship that is icy cannot produce warm-hearted children.

No parent is perfect. They may love their kids but overindulge their every excessive want as though a serious need. So many people have everything they could possibly want. Their parents love them but fail to teach them to care enough about those who struggle to put food on the table. The wisdom of love is sometimes not present with parents.

Children who repeatedly witness unkindness in their parents can become distant and alienated, and this can endure for years, contributing to antisocial or even violent behavior and struggles with depression.[85] Growing up in a dysfunctional, loveless family puts a child at a great disadvantage, but this can be ameliorated by the right spiritual community, the right mentors, warm friendships, a compassionate and understanding spouse, and counseling. In other words, it takes a lot. When parents are kind and loving to each other, life is generally so much better for their offspring who will usually grow up with more inner peace and psychological health.

The sociologist Sorokin studied the power of parents and families to generate kind and loving human beings:

> As a general rule the families with prevalent discordant relationships among their members, especially between husband and wife, where a newly born baby is unwelcomed, where it is deprived of the grace of love and from its early days breathes the poisonous air of discord and enmity in the relationship of the members of the family to itself and to one another; where there is neither a set of high values preached and practiced, nor wise and loving discipline combined with creative freedom; such families tend to produce morally erratic persons, little capable of self-control, selfishly irresponsible, careless of the interests and well-being of others, and frequently criminal or delinquent.[86]

Conversely, he showed that families characterized by high values, harmonious relationships, and wise love raise children who are more likely to be caring, compassionate, and giving.

A harmonious and healthy family unit is like money in the bank for children—a surefire means to experiencing and expressing kindness. Still, some of the kindest kids are raised by single parents, a grandparent, or someone who just takes a deep mentoring interest in them. How did they do it? What are the effective secrets to raising a kind child? And what has science said about this, if anything? It turns out that we know quite a lot about the "how to," and there are various practices that parents and other caregivers can implement.

Tested Approaches to Raising Kind Children

Develop a Family Mission Statement

In his influential and practical books, Thomas Lickona returns again and again to the importance of clearly stating the basics of a positive family culture. He recommends that every family develop a family mission statement and make it the cultural center of the family. The list should involve everyone and be intentional. "It lays the foundation for everything else you'll do to raise children of character. It becomes the point of reference in family life."[87] Discuss it and develop it as a young family. Have everyone sign it, agree to abide by it, and post it in the kitchen. A statement provides a foundation to build on when there is a behavioral problem or conflict. A sample family mission statement might look something like this:

We are kind, honest, and respectful.
We are patient and nonreactive.
We express gratitude.
We do our chores.
We eat as a family with TV, computers, and cell phones off.
It's better to be kind than to always be right.
We perform kind acts at home, in school, and in the neighborhood.
We put kindness before career.

With such a list, families with children are more likely to resolve behavioral problems when they arise. These are meant to be written in a list format and posted visibly where family members can gather round as needed for conversation.

Shared Family Values

Lickona also emphasizes how important it is to establish a list of family values agreed to by adults and children together and made visible in a gathering place in the home, perhaps taped to the refrigerator door or hung above the fireplace.[88] One value might be "Kindness first," and another "We do no harm," "Tell the truth," or maybe "Attitude of gratitude." Families need to be explicit about their agreed upon core values. That way, when inevitable behavioral issues minor and major come up, there is already a settled cultural identity in the family around which conversations can unfold and creative resolutions found. It is helpful when the family can support its listed values with a spiritual community that teaches love and kindness for young and old.

Family, Faith, and Community as the Centerpieces

Many negative cultural pressures must be resisted in the family. This is not easy today because behavioral standards and proper use of language have diminished. For example, the sit-down meal accompanied by saying grace and engaging in family conversation is, in many homes, overwhelmed by "grab-and-go" habits. Fast-food eating has invaded this special social and spiritual space of the family.

It has long been said that "the family that prays together stays together." But the antifamily philosopher Friedrich Nietzsche (d. 1900) observed a dissolution of the historical emphasis on the family. He was a philosopher, not a scientist, but prescient. He felt that selfish individualism was the dominant ethos and contrary to familial love and care. He predicted that in the twentieth century, "the family will slowly be ground into a random collection of individuals," haphazardly bound together "in the common pursuit of selfish ends," and in the common rejection of the structures and importance of family, faith communities, and civil society.[89] It would appear that much of what Nietzsche described has come true. If the sanctity of the family unit is a lost cause, it is one very much worth saving.

Convene Weekly Kindness Circle of Trust Meetings

Any family concerns should be resolved in a meeting. Anyone in the family can convene an emergency "kindness meeting." The best practice is to have weekly thirty- to sixty-minute meetings and allow people to talk about whatever has been on their minds over the past week. A Circle of Trust is a haven that affords the child the opportunity to feel protected when reflecting on an experience with another family member. This is a critical aspect of learning in an environment full of potential for negative and positive experiences.

Children as young as four or five can be involved in decisions on discipline by asking them this question: "What can you do to make up for that?" Parents must own up to their behavior, such as unnecessary screaming or moments of pointless anger. Parents can also suggest self-improvements. These meetings are a great chance to strengthen trust among family members, but guidelines that teach empathic communication must be followed:

1. Anyone in the group can bring up any case that engaged them emotionally and/or spiritually and perhaps left them with unresolved feelings. Examples of topics include suffering, compassion, guilt, loss, anger, fear, frustration, hostility, spirituality, integrity, hope, humiliation, inspiration, and good and bad role modeling.

2. Listen attentively, without interruption or distraction.
3. Respond generally and ask questions for clarification.
4. Focus on the speaker's feelings and experience.
5. Stay with the speaker. Do not redirect conversation or refocus on your own experience.
6. Offer confirmations rather than assertions or answers.
7. Respond, don't react.
8. Value moments of silence, especially after someone has spoken with heart and depth.
9. Be present emotionally.
10. Keep strict confidentiality. What is said in the room stays in the room.

Use the Right Style of Parenting

Authoritarian parents bark commands and threats and tend to scream. *Permissive* parents, who are affectionate but set little or no behavioral expectations for their children, are equally ineffective. The best style of parenting is *authoritative*, or characterized by confident authority and based on reasoning, fairness, love, and age-appropriate self-reliance. The authoritative parent draws attention back to the family mission statement and acts in a manner that is consistent with those values. Children get used to thinking in terms of the mission statement. Put kids on notice that their questionable behavior will be discussed at the next family meeting and encourage them to think about that ahead of time.

About 98 percent of parents in the United States indicate on surveys that, at some time or another, they have screamed at their kids.[90] Good parents try hard not to scream, but they sometimes do. It takes a lot of emotional self-awareness to control this perfectly.

Hang Rockwell's "The Golden Rule" (or Something Like It) in the Living Room

Samuel Oliner, one of the great sociologists of kindness who had been rescued from the Nazis during World War II as a child, studied the families that rescued Jewish children from the Holocaust. He discovered that most of the rescuers remembered their family had some rendition of the Golden Rule displayed in a socially central room, such as the living or dining room. When as children they did something, their parents would use the Golden Rule image or words as a reference point.

Manage Internet Screen Time

The American Academy of Pediatrics published an entire volume of the journal *Pediatrics* on the problem of too much screen time. Articles were based on studies that involved all the relevant divisions of the National Institutes of Health. Some of the findings linked excessive screen time with loss of one-on-one conversations and children with chronic irritability, poor focus, depression, meltdowns, and oppositional defiance.[91]

Neuroscientist Victoria Dunckley, in *Reset Your Child's Brain*,[92] recommends a four-week electronic fast that allows families to establish a culture of caring and of genuine communication. This may be difficult to implement with teens but can surely be managed with young kids.

Jonathan Haidt, social psychologist and author of *The Anxious Generation: How the Great Rewiring of Childhood Is Causing an Epidemic of Mental Illness*,[93] acknowledges, as we all must, that cell phones and computers do speed up work life for mature adults, but the flip side of this is that we are creating a new and largely unregulated world for children.

To get this under control, we all need to get creative. Here are some tips:

1. Advocate for phone-free grade schools and high schools.
2. Allow access to social media only after age fifteen.
3. Encourage kids to play outside in nature.
4. At times, let kids play without supervision, so they can learn to navigate the social world on their own and mature with some independence. Children need real-world relationships and independence to learn what it means to be caring and kind—and to make mistakes.
5. Do your best to maintain family rituals, like sit-down meals. What we eat matters a lot, but *how* we eat is at least as important. Lots of commonsense wisdom and virtue is transmitted at the table.
6. Get some help if family life becomes dominated by arguments over the use of technology.
7. Keep a nice dog around because when a child has a dog, they get outside more, they learn about real-life offline, and if mom and dad are screaming, that dog will try to lick a child's tears away.

Connect Kindness with Success over the Course of a Lifetime

Every parent needs to teach their kids that kindness should come before career. Teens can become ruthless in highly competitive high schools, especially if they have been taught that they either get admitted to elite institutions or fail forever. Sometimes parents even help their teens cheat to get into desired schools. I again recommend that every family mission statement include the phrase "kindness before career." Kindness will enhance career opportunities, as schools and employers look for someone who will be a good member of the community and a good colleague.

Put kindness alongside of career and communicate this with your own or your neighbor's children by role modeling. As children grow older and face the pressures of school and career competition, studies show that parents place less emphasis on kindness in high school and college. The focus shifts to "success," but the fact is that people who succeed best in life need the soft skills of kindness and emotional intelligence.[94]

In 2013 the Harvard Graduate School of Education launched the Making Caring Common Project, focusing on the importance of raising kind children who maintain empathy. The project's surveys indicated that the emphasis on kindness in kids diminished in high school as career goals came into dominance. Their suggestions for emphasizing kindness are similar to those offered by Lickona and my Institute for more than a decade, though with a bit more emphasis on the role of schools.[95]

My Institute has supported programs as early as 2005 on small group circles of trust, even in first and second grade, focused on virtues such as kindness, forgiveness, and generosity, as well as meditation. It turns out that these dynamics in early grade school tend to reduce aggressive behaviors and encourage better school performance.[96]

Our aspiration as parents and educators should always be "kindness builds career success." If people stray far from kindness, they will not find enduring or meaningful happiness in relationships, although they may have possessions galore. Kindness is at the center of the social and emotional intelligence of any fulfilling life and makes success across a lifetime possible.

Volunteer and Donate Together as a Family

Set time aside as a family and make volunteering a central weekly event—to local and global causes. An hour of volunteering per week is quite effective. As a family, debrief about the experience—perhaps over dinner. Ask everyone to say something about how they felt about their experience and what it meant to them.

Make Play a Priority

Raising children requires immense patience, humility, and loyalty. But the hard spiritual and moral work involved in raising kind children is, in any reasonably healthy family, balanced with joy and play.

THE KINDNESS QUOTIENT

The Kindness Quotient (KQ) is a relatively new term introduced in 2018 in *How the Power of Kindness Creates Success at Home, at Work and in the World*,[97] a book by child advocate Rhonda Sciortino, who recommends shifting from a focus on the intelligent quotient (IQ)—a measure of how smart someone is—and emphasizing the KQ—how kind a person is—as much or more than IQ. This happens mainly when people realize how much kindness is connected to happiness and success. KQ is part evaluation (quizzes and self-assessment measures) and part creating purpose by forming groups and receiving encouragement among other methods.

A high IQ is not bad unless it distracts young people and parents from KQ, which is what we really need for human progress. *A high IQ is a good thing only if KQ comes first.*

Beyond Parenting

Parents are not solely responsible for producing a caring child. Organizations and institutions must work hand in hand with parents. Schools do matter. The Montessori schools are useful because the older children actively tutor and help the younger ones. High schools often include, and sometimes require, service-learning opportunities, but I advocate adding courses in our high schools and universities—and even a major—in raising a kind child. Why don't we teach medical students, nurses, and clinical social workers how to achieve this goal? Pregnant women or couples could be referred to educational "how to" seminars. In earlier times, communities of faith provided "marriage preparation" instruction. But times have changed. We need new child-rearing classes held in spiritual communities and schools. We need these classes to be as common as Lamaze, which helps pregnant women build confidence in their ability to give birth.

We need to create environments in which being a person of love is modeled, expected, and rewarded in a fashion that is authoritative rather than authoritarian. Some of this already exists. Clubs can provide children with opportunities to learn the value of service. Churches and synagogues exhort and organize compassion and giving. Grandparents often provide the unconditional love that is sometimes a struggle for busy or overwhelmed parents.

To upgrade the future of humans, we need groups and institutions that supplement the family in the education of the heart. We need cultural systems that support the power of love in friendship, cooperation, and the pursuit of knowledge. We need our various religions to take love and compassion for all humanity much more seriously than they do now.

Society would save vast resources if we could learn how to raise kind children because they would be generally happier, healthier, and flourishing. By eliminating the stress of ACEs, which cause about half of all mental and physical illnesses across the life span, we would save unimaginable amounts in healthcare expenditures. We would see vast reductions in antisocial behavior, bullying, harassment, substance abuse, addiction, and incarceration. If we devoted a small fraction of what we spend on healthcare to teaching parents how to raise kind children, countless billions would be saved through illness prevention and the reduction of crime and wasted potential.

THE HAND THAT ROCKS THE CRADLE RULES THE WORLD

Truly, the hand that rocks the cradle rules the world. It creates a world of inner peace and love, or it creates a world of violence and hatred. And the physical health, happiness, psychological health, and even longevity of our children depend on our success in teaching them by example how to love others.

It is important to understand that for all my emphasis on parental love, I also assert that every teacher, babysitter, neighbor, relative, coach, minister, or literally any adult who spends any time around children, including of course the school bus driver, is absolutely able to contribute to the common goal of raising kind children. This is a job for everyone without exception. My wife is a devoted teaching assistant in the grade school in Setauket, New York, and earlier did this for years in Shaker Heights, Ohio. I have always felt that she does more to bring kindness into this world than I do because she influences children when they are earlier in their identity formation than the older students in medical schools. She practices kind giving every day, and on the weekends does a wonderful job designing elaborate bulletin boards.

Loving kindness is the one necessary ingredient for all inward growth. We human beings are standing on the threshold of a new era where growth in love will finally become the recognized primary goal of raising a child. Even from the very limited hedonic or utilitarian perspective, raising a child of love is good because that child will typically live a happier, more fulfilled, and healthier life. As Sorokin concluded after studying the lives of people widely recognized in their cultures for generous and compassionate behaviors, we can expect with high probability "a remarkable vitality, a long duration of life, an unperturbable peace of mind, and an ineffably rich happiness."[98] So, raising a child of goodness makes sense even within the framework of a culture that seems bent on emphasizing benefits to self. Most parents want their children to live happier, healthier, longer, and more peaceful lives.

It is a universal law of human nature that love begets love. When a parent creates a rapport of empathy, compassion, and love, a child will have the kindness and grace to bring positive change to the world. In a sense, a good parent must be like the good child psychiatrist who knows that empathy and understanding can prevent or resolve diverse psychiatric illnesses. Love heals. Unloved, unwanted, and rejected babies and children are like seeds planted on stones, and they will not grow in love. Children deprived of love in families and friendships will be much more likely to be unhappy and unproductive human beings. When this is coupled with our cultural sewer of violent videogames and websites, and with bullying in schools, the outcomes are predicable episodes of extreme violence.

I often think back to that suicidal student in Cleveland who had lost all confidence in the good side of human nature. We spoke for hours about all the great research my Institute had funded showing that kids are kind and compassionate by nature, but this wonderful inclination can be overwhelmed if parents push the wrong buttons by role modeling destructive emotions and creating trauma in their children.

I visited this student a few more times, bringing her some articles and books that told a more balanced and hopeful story of human nature. I gave her various kindness and compassion exercises that she could work with to guide her thinking, all of which seemed to help. She eventually went home to her family reasonably improved. We stayed in touch for a while. Her suicide attempt seemed to be based as much on her being confused by jaded and hopeless literature, research, and philosophy as in clinical depression and a challenging childhood. Ideas have consequences.

TIPS FOR RAISING KIND CHILDREN

- Encourage good parenting. We must examine ways in which kindness can be enhanced in couples to allow for more lasting unions and parenting styles that contribute to raising a caring child who in turn practices kindness.
- Talk to your school board. When schools are overwhelmed by bullying behaviors, the niche for kindness can be hard to sustain. So, schools must be highly intentional about an ethos of love and character education. In addition, curricula can be developed around literature that tells the story of kindness.
- Reform the media and related business leaders. Every parent these days fights a slow, relentless, and often painful battle in the home against the violence and hatred that seem to sell music and movies. Indeed, several parents have been killed by their teen children for disallowing X-Box computer game playing of a particularly violent game called *Halo*.
- Participate in a spiritual community. It is hard for parents and schools to sustain an ethos of love without spiritual

communities that provide social and moral support. We need strong communities of worship. Many studies show that religious people do on the whole tend to contribute more money to help others and engage in more volunteerism.
- Volunteer with your family, which can positively impact happiness and health. Many institutions depend on large numbers of volunteers these days.

My Morning Meditation

Every morning, I envision the faces of my kids, who are now young adults, with the help of a family photo taken fifteen years ago when we were all younger. I see the kindness and joy in their faces and imagine their inner child as inhabiting them even now many years later. I imagine them engaged in kind helping with kindness in their expressions and voices. I contemplate kindness in their hearts and visualize them doing kind acts. This helps me respond much more creatively if they get caught up in some untoward behavior, which is always possible. I envision myself as a good role model when they call on the phone, meaning that I am not going to say anything negative. I will nudge them a bit but without humiliating them. Carefrontation is a core aspect of parenting.

The Wheel of Love and Raising Kind Children

The Way of Carefrontation

Most of us can look back on our lives and identify parents and other adults who loved us actively and deeply. This love should not be confused with pampering or overindulging our children. We will not create caring children if we satisfy all their desires, fail to discipline them when they require it, and are otherwise permissive. Spoiling children and doting over them encourages irresponsibility and laziness. Love can be like medicine or poison. Unwise parental love can harm or destroy a young person.

I do not like the phrase "tough love" because it invites excess. Parents do, however, need to be experts at carefrontation, or the art of speaking the truth in a manner that builds up rather than tears down. Parents need to be both good models for love and good coaches. We need to create family cultures where we discuss concern for others and live by the principle of the Golden Rule.

The Way of Helping

One of the healthiest things we can do for a young person is to help them include kind giving activities in their lives. Such activities give rise to a set of emotions that are antithetical to hostility and self-preoccupation. This transformation of being and of doing seems to promote emotional and physical well-being and may well add some years of life. When we start young, this transformation has lifelong health benefits, but benefits can be derived whenever we start. Helping others provides meaning, a sense of self-worth, a social role, and health enhancement.

Concluding Thoughts

Parental love is a form of deep involvement and concern that, while capable of possessiveness and a lack of wisdom, is nevertheless at its best the closest thing we have here on earth to pure love. It is mostly unconditional and fully supportive, even when it must be firm. But it can also be abusive, as any pediatric social worker will attest. Therefore, society must sometimes intervene because love is the birthright of every human child and is needed from the moment of birth to the time of death. Love cannot help but enliven and expand the capacities of those who are loved to love in turn. Love begets love, hate begets hate.

Education in kindness begins at birth, and parents are the first and most important educators. The single most important educational function of parents is to draw out and nurture the potential in a child to become a loving human being. Everything else pales by comparison. Families and schools should have a common faith and purpose in the creation of love. The school too must become a setting as devoted to the raising of kind and loving children as are parents. Love is the supreme value, the highest good, the *summum bonum*, the fundamental dynamic of a good life from birth onwards. It cannot be overly permissive, and carefrontation is valid if a child is to have discipline and live a flourishing life. Carefrontation is scream free, and that is hard to achieve, but still a plausible goal. Parental love is neither permissive nor oppressive, but nurtures through providing direction in kindness.

CHAPTER 5

The Fifth Path: May You Know the One Mind

"My dear,

In the midst of winter, I found there was, within me, an invincible summer."

—Albert Camus

"We have to recognize that we are spiritual beings with souls existing in a spiritual world as well as material beings with bodies and brains existing in a material world."

—Sir John Eccles

Turning inwards in awareness of the One Mind in which we all share is central to the spirit of inner peace in so many great traditions, both Eastern and Western. This is a core theme in Buddhism and Hinduism, and in the Abrahamic traditions as well. It is a by-product or a side effect of the kind giving from the heart that does not bank on returns and is therefore invincible. It comes in part from the contentment that emerges from healing with kindness, from sticking with authentic callings, from raising kind children, from cherishing nature, from honoring the spirit of freedom. But if I had to state what has been most important in my own quest for inner peace, it is being aware of and connecting with the One Mind.

Knowing the One Mind or as it is often called the "Universal Mind" is a valuable treasure that, when at full strength, is undisturbed by the turbulent outside world. Yet this inner peace is at the same time fragile. We may feel inner peace, but at an existential level be nagged by the anxious feeling, described by the sages from Buddha in the East to Kierkegaard in the West, that our contentment today will be disrupted tomorrow, even if only by increasing awareness of mortality. Therefore, spiritual practices are essential to securing a more perfect unity between our particular minds and the Source of all mind—what is referred to as the One Mind of which each of our individual minds is an eternal part. In this context, inner peace is not a byproduct but the goal. Productive spiritual practices that bring us as individual minds into greater awareness of our oneness with the One Mind of which we are part is vital to inner peace.

What do I mean when I refer to the One Mind? What do I mean when I talk about individual minds, if such a possibility exists? And where does the brain fit into this picture?

More than a Lump of Protoplasm

Most of us in Western culture have been conditioned since high school to think of our minds as being synonymous with brain tissue, a local lump of protoplasm just behind the forehead. The brain, an organization of matter and cells, is remarkable—ensuring that our hearts beat, our lungs breathe, we can read the words on this page, and so much more—but it does not at all explain what Mind is. Although residing in the brain, Mind is so very different from tissue. Mind is pure Consciousness, or that which precedes Matter. Those acculturated to Hindu and Buddhist cultures think that Consciousness can only be understood as pure Mind, underivable from Matter.

Many of the best philosophers—and scientists—argue that there exists no compelling evidence that Mind can be derived from Matter anymore than blood can be derived from a stone. The Nobel laureate physicist Erwin Schrödinger famously described the Mysticism of the One Mind in the 1920s when he wrote, "There is obviously only one alternative, namely the unification of minds or consciousness. Their multiplicity is only apparent, for in truth there is only one Mind. To divide or multiply consciousness is something meaningless."[99] He also wrote that "the overall number of minds is just one . . . inconceivable as it seems to ordinary reason, you—and all other conscious beings as such—are all in all. Hence this life of yours which you are living is not merely a piece of the entire existence but is in a certain sense the *whole*; only this whole is not so constituted that it can be surveyed in one single glance."[100] At this level, we are one. So, when I help you, I help myself as well.

The Abrahamic faiths of Judaism, Christianity, and Islam at their highest expression are equally mystical with regard to the origin of our minds. Our conception of the physical material world as the ultimate reality has made it impossible for many of us to free our minds from this limited framework. But to understand One Mind, we must free ourselves from the belief that everything that exists is part of the material world.

The One and Only Mind

Each individual mind is a part of something infinite—part of the One Mind. In awareness of the One Mind within us, we discover inner peace at its manifestation, and this is the special, primary spiritual inner peace considered in this chapter. This is the peace that invades our consciousness as a spiritual energy, an energy that does not feel that it is coming from us. It is larger than we are, for it is the One Mind making itself felt irresistible. The One Mind *is Something More, a resource that can truly elevate the human soul above all circumstances bar none and upon which ultimate security depends.*

Within you is a seat of quiet spiritual security where the One Mind resides, responds, resolves all problems, and can be perfectly relied upon. We can always seek this rest and security within, but we will never find it in the outer material world at an invincible and lasting level. Clairvoyance, premonition, lives of astonishing creativity, and manifestations of Pure Unlimited Love at the level of great prophets, dreamers, artists, mystics, and saints are more reasonably explained with the idea of nonlocal Mind and the mystery of human connectivity in view. This more Eastern idea, along with the Christian idea of atonement, is at the core of my spiritual and moral identity.

The Nonlocal Mind and the Invasive Brilliance of the One Mind

Many thoughtful people believe that our individual minds are small drops of what my physician friends Larry Dossey and Deepak Chopra call "nonlocal Mind." This explains so many otherwise inexplicable mental phenomena, like dreams and intuitions that turn out to be premonitions, and creativity that seems to break into our minds from outside like an invasive brilliance as reported by many of the greatest inventors, scientists, and writers. By this theory, the individual mind is nonmaterial and continuous with a greater consciousness (aka, One Mind). In his wonderful book *One Mind: How Our Individual Mind Is Part of a Greater Consciousness and Why It Matters*,[101] Dossey describes our individual minds as underivable from matter and as both timeless and coextensive with the One Mind from which matter derives.

As a youth I had an experience of feeling this One Mind in action at Reed College in Portland, Oregon, in late January of 1970, thanks to a memorable phone call. From that experience I have never doubted that our minds are a mystery in their connectedness.

FEAR IN OREGON

The student coffeehouse at Reed College tended to fill up on the weekends. One cold, rainy Saturday night at about ten o'clock, I was drinking a cup of tea and talking with a few folks from my Alchemy 101 class on medieval science models of reality and quantum physics. In walked a wispy thin fellow with a mustache and lots of black leather clothing. He was red cheeked, his eyes were lit up, and he yelled flamboyantly across the room:

"Hey Reedies, my name is Andy from L.A. I have a new Harley-Davidson Shovelhead, the fastest motorcycle around. Who wants to take a ride?"

"I will," said a foolish youth. "Why not? I've never ridden on a motorcycle before." They went out into the parking lot, and the youth, who was at this moment perhaps more foolish than most young men, jumped on behind Andy.

To my surprise, Andy began screaming into the falling rain as he put his foot down hard on the gas. Within thirty seconds, we were doing one hundred miles an hour and headed for the highway, ignoring every red light and stop sign. We got out on the Pacific Coast Highway and skidded south on the slick road. It wasn't snowy or icy, but it was wet from the light cold rain and slippery with slush. I hung on for dear life with the rain now beating into my cold, reddened face, my wavy medium-brown hair streaming in the wind.

Andy seemed to feel more alive than ever. But for me, this ride felt like death itself. "Stop, let me off right now! You are going to get us both killed! It's too slippery! Bring me back now!" I demanded. But Andy only screamed all the louder into the wet darkness. I considered myself as good as gone. I began silently saying some prayers and anxiously chanting for divine intervention, my eyes closed tightly and the rain beating harder than ever against my red-cold cheeks.

"Lord, please get me off this bike alive, and I will be better and wiser for my whole life," I prayed. About a half hour later, Andy did a wild 180-degree flying U-turn, jumping the bike across the muddy midway, and finally headed back north toward Portland, hitting 140 miles per hour.

An hour later, Andy skidded back onto campus and pulled up to the exact same spot in front of the coffeehouse where he'd picked me up. I dizzily stepped off, totally shaken, while Andy laughed like the devil before skidding into the night with his engine blasting. I walked slowly back across the bridge over the ravine to my dormitory. I stumbled into the common room, drenched, shivering, and feeling lucky to be alive.

Just as I entered the building, the pay phone on the wall started ringing. I felt pushed a little from behind my right shoulder by some sort of energy, turned to look, but there was nothing visible there. The energy felt real enough to make me walk over to the phone and pick it up.

That call, about 11:00 p.m. Pacific time, came from my distressed mom in New York, where it was 2:00 a.m.

"You're alive! I had the most terrible dream that you were about to die. I was sound asleep, and I woke up with this shock and fear in my soul, and I felt for sure that you were dead," she gasped.

I explained what happened, adding that the driver was probably drugged up. "His eyes were on fire like Roman candles in the dark, and he must have enjoyed freaking me out. He was screaming and laughing like the devil. How did you know this clear over in New York?"

"Mothers just feel these things. They know. It's a mystery."

"But Mom, you're almost three thousand miles away. It isn't possible."

"Distance doesn't matter," said Mom, an Irish Catholic mystic herself. "Moms just know. The Mind is such a mystery," she continued. "Our Magee family in Ireland used to have premonitions, one of which saved your great-grandfather from the English when they were coming to hang him for going to a forbidden Catholic Mass. His wife told him to leave home after her dreamy premonition. So, he hid with his son in a cave along the Donegal coast for a few days and then walked to Galway to board a ship. The English really did come to hang him, but he was gone. They had booked passage on a boat for New York. That son, John Magee, became a harpooner out of Sag Harbor, where he was buried in the village graveyard."

Mom, known as Molly Magee, was prayerful and took dreams seriously. She was surely going to make that call to me, as she was nudged to do so by something that invaded her consciousness.

I went upstairs to my dorm suite, calmer but still shaken, and fell asleep thinking that a mom's mind is good evidence of a collective Universal Mind that goes beyond biology, time, and place. Carl Jung had the Universal Mind in view when he wrote about a collective unconscious and the "uncaused causality" of synchronicity. When we experience this Oneness, we sense that we are more cherished by the universe because perfectly timed events and interactions take place so improbably that they could not be random. We do have to notice them, and not everyone does.

There was something about Mom's mind that night that had to transcend the cells and tissue of her material individual brain and that could connect her with the boy three thousand miles away and over the Rocky Mountains. I thought it comforting that a mother's worried love allowed her nonlocal consciousness to manifest across those miles in its connection with the One Mind. In some way, it seems that the energy of such relatively pure love transcends all space and place and responds to feelings of anxiety for those who are so deeply cared about when imperiled. Maybe this connectivity becomes most evident only when intensified and guided by the energy of pure love, which is intense.

Eastern spirituality views the One Mind or Consciousness as "god," as the Supreme Source of everything through some sort of Big Bang. Because our individual minds are a gift and ever a small part of this One Mind, they are nonlocal. Hindu scriptures say there is a dimension of our minds that is beyond place and time. They call it "the Supreme." Hanging around with the poet Robert Bly at Reed had made such a Jungian idea easy for me to take seriously. Running across a very young Steve Jobs there helped too. His spiritual leanings were clear to all, as his favorite book was *The Autobiography of a Yogi*.

IT DIDN'T ADD UP

In 1912, Srinivasa Ramanujan, a mathematician from India with no formal training, sent samples of his equations to the great Cambridge mathematician G. H. Hardy, who immediately invited Ramanujan to become a fellow at the Trinity College, Cambridge. During his short lifetime (1887–1920), Ramanujan produced by sheer inspiration 3,900 original and often brilliantly unconventional equations—most of which have been proven correct.

Ramanujan claimed to have received many insights while kneeling before Namagiri, a Hindu goddess. He would jot them down in the dirt with his finger as he knelt and come back a few hours later to copy them into his notebooks. He said that Namagiri also appeared in his dreams and showed him these mathematical equations, which he would write down when he awoke (*The Man Who Knew Infinity*, a motion picture, tells the story of Ramanujan).

No one at Cambridge could nudge Ramanujan to formally "prove" his equations for he found proofs to be boring. After all, he knew the formulae came from the Supreme Mind. Ramanujan was able to receive the creativity of the One Mind from his place of deep meditational inner peace. He received these equations from the infinite reservoirs of the One Mind, the original creative genius of the universe. He felt that all he did was to *accept* what the Supreme wanted to bring forth through him.

Ramanujan died at an early age in India, but his three groundbreaking mathematical notebooks are displayed in a glass case in the middle of the Trinity College Library, where his statue can also be viewed. The equations and formulae in these notebooks were mostly the work of an untrained late adolescent, but it's widely acknowledged that they form the basis for much of quantum physics and many other modern advances.[102]

Intuition Is Immaterial

A Mind is something that we cannot understand fully. It remains a mystery. The science of Mind is opaque. No scientist has yet to show that you can get Mind from Matter.

We do understand that Matter is local, and the brain exists in this place, at this time. But Mind is not restricted to locality, and the miles between New York and Oregon mean nothing to it. Mind is something distinct. It's not physical but spiritual. Indeed, it is more likely that all Matter and Energy derive from the One Mind that precedes and underlies all being and Ultimate Reality. Einstein and Oppenheimer understood this as unproven yet still very plausible. The latter was a careful student of the ancient scriptures underlying Hinduism, the *Upanishads*.

Materialists certainly reject this argument, but the nonmaterialists are not backing down. These transpersonal psychologists study the connection between the self and a higher consciousness. They believe, as do I, that human experience can extend beyond the ego, reach the transcendental (awareness of the One Mind), and imbue our lives with love, compassion, meaning, and inner peace. Transpersonal psychology is not yet mainstream, but it is making immense gains and goes back to the great Harvard psychologist and religious philosopher William James.

Consider those intuitive moments when you just "know" something, as if tapping into a higher level of knowledge. Consider the synchronistic encounters that seem to show up directly in answer to a prayer. Consider the surprising premonitions that people have and the dreams that turn out to be accurate. Consider the significant numbers of great creative people in the sciences and arts who have worked hard to master their endeavors but who also describe their most innovative breakthroughs in terms of a visionary moment when they felt peaceful within a Oneness. Mihaly

Csikszentmihaly, my Hungarian psychology professor at Chicago, described in his great study of flow states how people in creative heights touch the mystic sense of being beyond time and place.[103]

The materialists would say that our minds are walled off from other minds or from the divine Mind. Fences, yes, but walls never. As the Hindus say, *Atman (self) = Brahman (Godhead)*. We each have within us some small drop of the Supreme's eternal essence and therefore are one "stuff" with the divine, like a drop of water in the sea.

"Something there is that does not love a wall," as Frost wrote, and that will not allow us to be walled off.[104] But waste-high fences are good enough to keep us distinct as individuals despite being coextensive with the same original One Mind.

The Christian version of this is nicely captured by St. Paul: "Do you not know that you are God's temple and that God's Spirit dwells within you?"[105] Tolstoy's favorite biblical verse was, "The kingdom of God is within you."[106]

The Heart of Religion Survey

I need to add a little more to the earlier mention of our national survey of the experience of divine love. Many people in the United States are aware of the One Mind, otherwise known as "Universal Mind" or God. In our widely reviewed Heart of Religion Survey (2013)—a scientific survey of randomly selected US adults—Harvard's Matthew T. Lee, the now deceased Margaret Poloma, and I tried to provide a valid portrait of the American perceptions and experiences of divine love, both directly and through others. Respondents were interviewed by telephone in English or Spanish in the fall of 2009. The results can be generalized to the vast majority of Americans, with a margin of error of plus or minus 2.9 percentage points.

Here are the stats for the question "Do you feel God's love for you directly?" ("N" represents the number of people who answered as indicated):

Never / not asked: 17.4% (N = 210)
Once in a while: 13% (N = 156)
Some days: 10.5% (N = 126)
Most days: 14.1% (N = 170)
Every day: 35.6% (N = 427)
More than once per day: 9.3% (N = 112)

To be a little more precise, we learned that about 81 percent of American adults feel God's love directly, at least once in a while. Almost half (45 percent) of all Americans feel God's love at least once a day, 9 percent feel God's love more than once a day, and eight out of ten have this experience at least "once in a while." Almost half (48 percent) of the respondents who had a strong sense of purpose directly experienced God's love daily or more, as compared with the 14 percent who had a strong sense of purpose but never experienced divine love.

It is encouraging that about 81 percent of Americans, many of them no longer religious in terms of institutional membership, self-report experiencing a loving Source that empowers them to express the spirit of creative love and benevolent purpose, or what we refer to in chapter 3 as Callings. Of those, 35.6 percent experience this sensation once a day, and 9.3 percent "more than once per day."[107]

Despite our culture's obsession with wealth, power, status, and celebrity, millions of Americans are quietly engaged in a deeply spiritual struggle to wake up from petty selfishness and embrace a life of inner peace, benevolence, and compassion. The highest expressions of kindness, hope, creativity, joy, truth, progress, and peace flow from our inner essence of spirit; failing to connect with it confines us to the limited consciousness of the physical body and results in greed, attachment, ego, arrogance, bitterness—a general and persistent state of unhappiness.

WAVES OF BRILLIANCE

Hans Berger (1873–1941) was nineteen in 1893 when he fell off a horse during cavalry training with the German army and was nearly trampled by a horse-drawn canon. The driver of the canon halted just in time, but the young Berger was badly shaken. On that same day, his sister, many miles away, had a bad feeling that her brother Hans was in great danger or even dead. She convinced her father to send him a telegram asking if Hans was all right. To young Hans, this eerie timing was not mere coincidence. He called this later an episode of "spontaneous telepathy," for he was convinced that he had somehow transmitted his thoughts of mortal fear to his sister.

Hans went into psychiatry at the University of Jena, Germany, on a quest to understand how thoughts could travel between people. His goal was to discover the physiological basis of "psychic energy." He did not find the answer, but he did invent the electroencephalogram (EEG), a device to measure electrical activity in the brain, and first used it successfully in 1924.

Berger knew nothing about electricity or mechanics and was mocked when he shared that the brain had a "rhythmic oscillation" present when subjects were still. But the Nobel laureate Edgar Adrian of Cambridge University confirmed that the EEG measured what came to be known as the alpha wave rhythm, and the two of them began to publicize the idea and the evidence. Berger's theory of alpha waves measurable by the EEG had finally been recognized in 1937 at an international forum and started to be used to diagnose epilepsy in the United States, England, and France by 1938 when Berger was sixty-five. A little later, he wrote about how brain waves could not explain his communication to his sister, for waves could not travel far enough to reach her.

> But the byproduct of Berger's quest to explain his sister's knowledge of his fear was the development of the EEG, which is nowadays an indispensable clinical tool when diagnosing not only epilepsy but sleep apnea, brain tumors, and much more. No one thinks that the alpha wave rhythm is a crazy idea, and they are eponymously called "Berger waves."[108]

INTO THE MYSTIC: THE MYSTICISM OF MIND, HEART, AND NATURE

Mysticism is the experience of becoming one with the Absolute. This experience can occur through the feeling of being a channel of the One Mind in terms of concepts, ideas, and what the Greeks called *nous*, or divinely inspired thoughts. I refer to this as One Mind Mysticism, or OMM. This is what much of this chapter focuses on.

But mysticism makes itself known not only through the Mind but also the Heart. Some mystics, such as Mother Theresa, St. Francis of Assisi, and Mother Ann Lee of the Shakers, were mystics of the heart. The Mysticism of the One Original Heart is the mysticism of Pure Unlimited Love. Many who take seriously the experience of One Mind are also taken up into the experience of One Heart. Many mystics are heart-love centered in their theological writings, with metaphors of heart and love everywhere in their language. This One Heart love is not mere human emotion but something much larger. The idea of *feeling* invaded by a spiritual energy larger than self has been powerfully described by poet W. H. Auden in his reflection of an evening on the grounds of a prep school (north of Oxford) where he was teaching:

> One fine night in June 1933 I was sitting on a lawn after dinner with three colleagues, two women and one man. We liked each other well enough, but were certainly not intimate friends, nor had any one of us a sexual interest in another. Incidentally we had

not drunk any alcohol. We were talking casually about everyday matters when, quite suddenly and unexpectedly, something happened. *I felt myself invaded by a power which, though I consented to it, was irresistible and certainly not mine.* For the first time in my life I knew exactly—because thanks to the power, I was doing it—what it means to love one's neighbor as oneself. I was also certain that, though the conversation continued to be perfectly ordinary, that my three colleagues were having the same experience. (In the case of one of them, I was later able to confirm this.) My personal feelings toward them were unchanged—they were still colleagues, not intimate friends—*but I felt their existence as themselves to be of infinite value and rejoiced in it.*[109]

Auden is describing something more than a transformation of intellect. He is speaking here of a Pure Love that is ultimately identifiable with a mystical "invasion." He feels "their existence as themselves to be of infinite value" and rejoices in it. *Pure love feels the awesome value of each and every person, without exception.*

Finally, there is the mysticism of nature. One rarely finds a meditation or prayer center that does not include a wind chime or a little flow of water. This is the subject of the next chapter, but the Mysticism of Nature has to be included thirdly, even though it has been somewhat de-emphasized in the Abrahamic traditions. This form of mysticism has been highly popularized through the writings of great modern theologians such as Thomas Berry in his landmark book *The Dream of the Earth*, as well as Merton, Gandhi, Gary Snyder, Rebecca Solnit, and others who identify with the legacy of St. Francis of Assisi. As Berry wrote, "Teaching children about the natural world should be treated as one of the most important events in their lives. Children need a story that will bring personal meaning together with the grandeur and meaning of the universe."[110]

Berry also wrote: "We are talking only to ourselves. We are not talking to the rivers, we are not listening to the wind and stars. We have broken the great conversation. By breaking that conversation, we have shattered the universe. All the disasters that are happening now are a consequence of that spiritual autism."[111]

Walk in nature. This is not a luxury but an inner peace and healing necessity. Stop, look, listen, and touch at a slow pace. Beauty is everywhere, as are the healing emotions of awe, wonder, and peace. Stay close to nature every day for at least a while. Try to stay silent, if possible, and breathe deeply. Nature and the awe it can inspire make us feel smaller, like in a Japanese painting where the mountainside of nature is everywhere, and human beings are small, barely discernible figures. This universe is vast; we are not. But we are an important part of something much bigger.

HOW DOES IT FEEL?

Folksinger and songwriter Bob Dylan was often referred to as a prophet, but he never thought of himself as such. *A Complete Unknown*, the 2024 movie about the young Dylan, portrays his incredible dreamy nights of writing verse, when he often felt that the words were not coming from him so much as through him. He later acknowledged that those early years were creatively unique.

When journalist Ed Bradley interviewed Dylan in 2004 on **60 Minutes**, Bradley asked Dylan where his words came from. He said he wrote right out of "that well-spring of creativity.... I don't know how I got to write those songs... those early songs were almost magically written.... Try to sit down and write something like that, there is a magic to that, and it's not Siegfried and Roy magic. It's a different kind of penetrating magic.... I did it at one time."[112]

He used the word "destiny" a lot and associates it with what the higher unseen has in mind for him. That early period in his life as a songwriter in New York City was filled with quasi-mystical creative sparks. Years later, the spark returned, but it was not quite the same.

The Point of Religion

The One Original Mind explains so much direct universal experience that is sometimes obscured by human doctrines. These are our best guideposts toward the essence of original inner peace.

If dogmas could all give way to states of quietude and awareness of the One Mind, we might know relief from the conflicts of the world. Psalm 46:10 captures this simply: "Be still, and know that I am God." The goal of religion is to still the constant turbulence and restlessness that naturally exists in the human Mind—what Buddhists and Hindus refer to as "monkey Mind"—when separated from its powerful center of the One Mind within by direct perception. Popular among many people today are methods of meditation that focus directly on the inexhaustible energy of the universal consciousness that promotes not just inner peace but world peace.

When virtue declines greatly, as it does in periods of civil unrest—when people are alienated from true community, wisdom, pure love, kindness, equal regard, and compassion—some new teaching always appears. The new teacher demonstrates full Consciousness—compassion, healing kindness, love for nature, as kindness for all humanity without exception. We may yet see the end of the modern world, but these things will allow for the beginning of a new world.

THE DIVINE SPARK AND DEEPLY FORGETFUL PEOPLE

For many years, one of my callings has been to provide respite care for family caregivers of people with dementia. I recall vividly a drive to Mount Vernon, Ohio, with the distinguished Harvard and Case Western neurologist Joseph M. Foley, MD, where we visited a hospital for older adults with various memory disorders. We entered a large ward for people with Down syndrome, almost all of whom are diagnosed with Alzheimer's disease by age fifty. They were quite unruly and agitated. In walked several Hindu nurse aides and every one of the forty-plus residents in the unit quieted down within a couple of minutes, especially after the aides sang a beautiful mantra for them.

Joe and I took two of those aides to lunch at a pizza place near Kenyon College, and we asked them how it was that they were able to bring such peace to those residents. They answered "Namaste," which is an Indian greeting. It means "I honor the divine in you/us, and in myself." They waxed eloquently about how people with memory impairment are still fully worthy of our respect and best care because they always have within them that divine spark.

Dr. Foley, who had arrived decades earlier at Case Western School of Medicine to chair the department of neurology after cochairing at Harvard for years, was a Roman Catholic and I am Episcopalian. Yet we shared a great deal in common with these aides, including their sense of a spiritual essence in all people without exception, including those with cognitive challenges. This idea of the origin of our minds in the One Original Mind intrigued us both. for it meant that no matter how compromised linear reasoning might become, we are all always of infinite eternal value.

ACHIEVING AWARENESS OF THIS MYSTERY

We humans have gotten away from our original state of inner peace, a peace many of us felt in the arms of our loving mothers when we first opened our eyes. To enter into the state of this mystery, one must practice quiet awareness centered on the inner being while paying no heed to the commotion of the outer world, especially in our highly fragmented and complex technological society. But what to do? There are so many spiritual techniques from various traditions to help us develop this inward awareness.

One shoe does not fit all. Many people relax their muscles from head to toe, starting with the areas between the eyes. They focus on deep slow breathing, usually with eyes closed. Within a few minutes, attention is solely on the inner Mind and the outer word seems to be less central. They feel that they move beyond body and matter to pure light and feel an inner peace.

Meditating is listening to the One Mind; praying is speaking to it. A key to prayer or meditation is to be at one with your peaceful soul and its connectivity with this Source. From this place within, we can envision loving goals and achieve a oneness with a power for goodness that is greater than ourselves.

You were made for this ocean of stillness and peace, where you can feel comforting love. Attachment to the inner being removes bitterness over past events, washes away impurities, and allows a flow of pure love. Rumination, hostility, and self-destructive tendencies recede. We enter a state of awareness—of pure love, peace, and freedom. Unblocked by the burden of guilt, unworthiness, and judgments, total acceptance is made possible by this soothing One Mind of which we are a part. Inner peace in the very deepest sense comes from gaining confidence in this pure love.

The great spiritual figures of all traditions counsel us to meditate, chant, or pray in the early mornings, before the world impinges on us. When we awaken early, we are not yet caught up in chronological time, and we may also feel beyond place. This is a prime time to find an inner peace with a Source that can infuse our souls with a deeper and more powerful love than our own—the energy of Pure Love. We can meditate on a passage such as, "I feel pure unlimited love in my heart." This can be repeated in quiet moments during the day when we can stop, look at ourselves, and listen to our hearts. The ancient mystics stated that we can connect with the One Mind in this flow beyond the grasp of time and place because it is also beyond time and place.

Feeling the presence of this Source is necessary if we are to be consistent instruments of peace, fully sow love over hatred, reliably sustain realistic hope over despair or mere dispositional optimism, focus healing light energies in times of darkness, or find deep joy despite sadness. Diving deep into meditation and prayer opens the door to this Source, which is always present but often goes unnoticed and unappreciated.

INNER PEACE MEDITATION

Close your eyes and clear your mind. Breathe deeply several times and relax your body bit by bit from the forehead to the toes. Place your middle fingers on the middle of your forehead above the eyes, pause there, and quietly say "One Original Mind" several times. Then let your hand descend to your heart region, pause there, and quietly say "One Original Heart" several times. Then let both your hands settle in the middle of your chest and, breathing out, repeat "One Original Peace." Feel that synergistic peace of Mind and heart and repeat this exercise anytime that you feel that you are being drawn down into the spiraling negative vortex of destructive emotions.

Pure Unlimited Love is not above the world but an energy to transform the world that lies within every human being without exception, although we must become aware of it and cultivate it. *In a simple formula: One Original Mind (OOM) + One Original Heart (OOH) = One Original Peace (OOP).*

I pause and do this meditation during the day. We all need some sort of inner practice to maintain our true human being. In grasping this state of One Original Peace, we are embracing the best in all faith traditions, which is visible once various dogmas are peeled away.

The Importance of Inner Integrity

Inner peace is in significant part the fruit of moral integrity, of being true to conscience and fully "integrated" with it. Sometimes people will pull us in directions that violate our conscience and deepest values, and we may feel divided and unfaithful to our inner being. Conscience is not simply derived from social pressures but directly from the One Mind within, because conscience can break through to new levels that make clear our moral blind spots. Within this One Mind are the virtues of truthfulness, generosity, kindness, honesty, and humility. Immense internal stress is the inevitable result of a divided heart, one that contradicts the One Mind within us.

All the great spiritual traditions understand conscience as a manifestation of an Inner Light. Inner peace of conscience arises from being aware of the One Mind within. We can achieve inner peace and tranquility by consistently following moral conscience—sticking with the higher self, having a unified heart and Mind, and being careful to choose virtuous friends and communities. When we do anything that seriously violates our inner being, we feel it for a long time, but the Oneness heals. Love always heals.

Eve of Destruction

The world is replete with people who, disconnected from the One Mind, seek annihilation of self or others or both. This can be particularly harmful when these individuals are powerful leaders. We have seen leaders on every continent wanting to create empires and engage in every war theatre possible. In the process, they have engaged in genocide and other atrocities incomprehensible to most people. Some leaders are best described as warmongers—politicians and dictators who profit from destruction. Bob Dylan called them "masters of war" in his song of the same name released just at the start of the Vietnam War.

Human history has thus far manifested equal measures of peaceable kindness and horrific hatred. Historically, the warmongers and others who would hurt members of their own species to support a destructive, human-generated ideology have felt threatened by people who demonstrate a love for all humanity—those working in harmony with the One Mind. On some level, they must understand the power of the One Mind, for they go so far as to assassinate these individuals—for example, Gandhi, Lincoln, King, Rabin, and Bhutto. Those souls who take this devilish route prefer a false Oneness of exclusion and annihilation, which is manifested through snobbery, injustice, and genocide. False Oneness eliminates those who are different for ethically and spiritually unacceptable reasons of race, ethnicity, color, creed, class, intellect, gender, and age.

Those who have devoted their lives to true and inclusive Oneness have cultivated an inner peace, despite their varied beliefs, backgrounds, and spiritual practices. In simplicity they rose above sensate materialism, or the belief that reality is derived from the physical, to focus on the deeper things we all hold within our minds and hearts—kindness, humility, forgiveness, peace, and benevolence. These martyrs all developed an inner peace that withstood the assault of adversaries so successfully that someone felt they had to be killed.

More people now understand "spirituality" and One Mind thought today, but there are those who are empty spiritually, so devoid of purpose or community or meaning that they will shoot into a classroom or store full of people in a meaning-seeking moment of destruction that culminates in their own deaths. This is now part of our American culture.

American culture is now a *danse macabre*, or "dance of death," in which rampant destruction is commonplace.

Sociologists refer to this dance of death as "edgework," or taking risks for the fun of it—including risks that may result in one's death. It is the manifestation of a soul already living on the edge of self-annihilation, a soul void of any meaningful connections to family or community or even self. When a teenager walks into a grocery store or a school with the intention of gunning down as many people as possible and eventually takes their own life or when someone shoots their arm full of heroin knowing that it might be laced with fentanyl or worse, we might call it "Thanatos," or a death drive. The more current term is "edgework." The human condition, deprived of consolation and a sense of divine presence, devolves into this indignity.

It is time for change. There is an invincible love within us all, no matter how hard the world pushes against it. When we feel this love, it is a sign of the One Heart within. The narratives of love practiced by solid families and faith communities can push against the violent media and video games encouraged by an empty materialistic culture.

Most people want a stable world, a world shrouded in outer peace. This state is possible, but it can only be reached when the majority of people on our seven continents feel an enduring and deep peacefulness within their own hearts and minds—when they become aware of the One Mind and cultivate inner peace.

One Mind, One Love, One Peace

The One Mind was here first and is the metaphysical glue that holds everything together. There is agreement about this Pure Love, which is the One Mind and One Heart that unites and subsumes all individual minds. The transcendentalists of Boston, such as philosopher-essayist Ralph Waldo Emerson, wrote of the universal Mind as the Over-Soul, which is that unity . . . within which every man's particular being is contained and made one with all others.

The Chandogya Upanishad (c. 600 BCE), an ancient Hindu sacred text, includes the famous phrase, *tat tvam asi*, or "thou art that," as an expression of the nature of Brahman, or the Supreme Reality. "That" refers to the Supreme Mind that is both the highest and also the inmost. "Allah" is used by Arabic speakers of all the Abrahamic faiths (including Christianity and Judaism) to refer to God and is based on the word for "I AM," as is Yahweh in Hebrew. It is not a name at all. Many spiritual people refer to the One Mind as "the Universe" or "Universal Mind," which also suggests something too profound to be named. It is good to give people and dogs names. It is bad to give "God" names, because people get too attached to these names and get into fights over which one is best. The Source does not care about names. Hence, "I AM."

Finding the Rose in the Desert

The Bible predicts that "the desert shall rejoice and blossom as the rose" (KJV).[113] Will we ever manage to find the rose in the desert when up against the internal negative emotional pressures created by a world of human de-dignification? Can our inner being, our soul, still be glad in the wilderness? Can we escape *The Wasteland* that T. S. Eliot described in one of the most famous poems of the twentieth century? His imagery of stony rubbish, where barbarity is rudely forced on all and anything truly meaningful is cancelled and silenced, seems appropriate in our materialist age. We share William Butler Yeats's question, "And what rough beast, its hour come round at last, Slouches towards Bethlehem to be born?"[114]

Can we find the rose in the desert of our own empty hearts, one that is a source of fulfillment?

Tips to Knowing the One Mind

- Let it be. The answers to your problems and distresses are there within the One Mind and will flow to you when the time is right. This does not mean that these assurances and solutions will always come to you in a still small voice. Rather, they may more commonly come through other people. This is referred to as "synchronicity," and most Americans have had such experiences. In moments of need, just the right person at the right time with the right wisdom and tone tells you just the thing you need to hear, often in answer to a prayer.
- Slide deeply into a state of *complete repose*, with a Mind emptied of thought and chatter. This can be accomplished by closing your eyes and beginning to breathe deeply ten or twelve times as you relax your body more and more with each breath.
- Keep an open Mind and heart to continuity with the One Mind and the One Heart that are the Ultimate Reality of the universe and within each of us.
- Envision the Wheel of Love, or better yet, sketch one out and tape it to something so you can see it as you contemplate the images of the primary people you know you will encounter today. Gaze at them remotely and trust your empathic feelings about what they might need today from the various expressions of love. Feel their presence in your heart and project love.
- Say to yourself, "I am this day the instrument of inner peace for everyone I meet."

My Morning Meditation

Before doing my morning meditation, I slow my mind and empty it of any chattering or thoughts. I focus on my breath, which frees me from focusing on thoughts, or what the Buddhists call "monkey Mind." I close my eyes and relax or soften all my muscles so that tensions disappear. The goal is to bring all thoughts to a hard stop. For the One Mind to break through, to invade and uplift me, I need to make space in my mind.

In addition to thoughts about schedules and to-do lists, our little minds are usually jam-packed with judgments, biases, assumptions—millions of little bits of junk that have been poured into them. It is good to sit in silence and just take in the gentle quiet.

The Wheel of Love in the Pursuit of the One Mind

The Way of Compassion

I have come to believe that all human beings are suffering, some more than others, all the time. It is a struggle not to give in to the challenges and adversities of life that we all encounter. Compassion begins with the recognition of suffering in ourselves and in those around us and incudes a desire to diminish that suffering. When we meditate and pray for those who are suffering, we find some inner peace. But when we alleviate suffering with wise words, the healing arts and medicines, and the cultivation of hope, we can know the meaning of love. When we make time to know the One Mind and feel the One Heart, we are refreshed, like a rose in the desert (Isa. 35). No matter how dry that desert might be, we can be enlivened by being aware of and experiencing our oneness with the divine.

The Way of Forgiveness

Awareness of the One Mind leads to forgiveness as it pushes aside the bitterness within our hearts and minds, putting end to cold rumination. Bitterness of heart and Mind fights against inner peace and gives rise to isolation and destruction. Forgiveness allows inward freedom from all those who would humiliate and de-dignify us. Forgiveness makes fertile ground in the soul for feeling the presence of the One Mind and the One Heart. Many books are written about the "how-to" of forgiveness, about what it is and is not. All of this is important to spiritual life.

The Way of "Carefrontation"

When as are aware of the One Mind of which all minds are a part, we can "carefront" our inner being and our soul—that center within where our profound feelings, emotions, personal journey, and attitudes come together sometimes in celebration and sometimes in destruction of self and others. These elements must be released through techniques like deep breathing and through prayer and participation in positive communities and their spiritual practices.

The Way of Helping

Many of the great mystics who experienced inner peace were great builders of communities in which spiritualty was primary. They were often monkish and developed disciplines and rules to live by (as in the case of the Benedictine's Rules), and these gave rise to new civilizational eras. One need only visit Kyoto to see how essential Zen Buddhist creativity was to the architecture and culture of Japan. Building community and connection flows naturally from the One Mind that leads to inner peace.

The Way of Mirth

A big part of inner peace is levity. English author and philosopher G. K. Chesterton wrote, "Angels can fly because they can take themselves lightly, devils fall because of their gravity."[115] Love and spirituality and uplifting mirth are intertwined. I personally have lived a relatively creative life while navigating the many adversities along the paths. At a certain level, I take my work as a writer and teacher very seriously, but I also do not take myself too seriously. I never want to forget the kindness of a smile or the way in which a dad joke brings levity into my family, my workplace, my soul. Laughter drives the darkness out of our lives internally and communally. It is part of my tool kit for expressing love and finding inner peace.

The Way of Loyalty

Bill Wilson, cofounder of Alcoholics Anonymous, was not previously a believer when he claimed he saw and felt a white light, which he perceived as the presence of a divine love, or the One Mind. This occurred in his hospital room at a New York detox center on his fourth day of treatment: "It seemed to me, in the Mind's eye, that I was on a mountain and a wind not of air but of spirit was blowing. And then it burst upon me that I was a free man."[116]

After that spiritual experience of December 14, 1934, Bill never drank again, and Alcoholics Anonymous (AA) was born. How many millions of alcoholics over the decades have been saved from illness and death by virtue of joining the AA communities? Bill had found his Divine Source, and it led to inner peace. He was loyal to his commitment to help free others from alcoholism, and he realized that he had to be kind to be well.

The Way of Creativity

The highest forms of creativity flow from experiencing the One Mind. So many creative people feel that their moments of deep creativity were, to use Auden's metaphor, not so much from them as through them (see page 140). Creativity, freedom, and love are the essential features of the divine Mind.

CONCLUDING THOUGHTS

As many great spiritual traditions propose, "Mind *before* Matter." Inner peace can in part derive from kind giving, healing with kindness, following your callings, raising kind children, cherishing the gift of nature, and honoring the spirit of freedom, but in this fifth chapter we focused on the ultimate inner peace as derived from awareness of our oneness with the One Mind. If only each of us would *notice* and *feel* the Oneness, Inner—and Outer—Peace would rise to the highest levels.

CHAPTER 6

The Sixth Path: May You Cherish the Gift of Nature

> "Teaching children about the natural world should be seen as one of the most important events in their lives."
>
> —Thomas Berry

> "Our task must be to free ourselves from this prison by widening our circle of compassion to embrace all living creatures and the whole of nature and its beauty."
>
> —Albert Einstein

In my work, I've traveled a lot over the years. No matter what town I'm in, I usually seek out a meditation center to find inner peace in the quiet. Wherever I go, I can count on finding a sculpted stream of water, some wind chimes, and likely some beautiful plants. This is, of course, by design. The beauty and mystery of nature—even when indoors—has the power to fill us with awe and bring heart and mind to a peaceful space.

Being with nature empties me of the flow of mundane and worldly thoughts that make me anxious. When I listen to the stream of water and the wind chimes, the clutter drifts away, and I find myself wanting to be mindful and to pray, alone or with others. Nature is a conduit for finding inner peace.

Nature is not God, not something to be worshipped, but something to be cherished as a gift from the Supreme Being. Nature is large, and we are a part of it biologically, just as our minds are spiritually part of the One Mind. Nature nurtures the soul and eases us into simply being instead of always doing. Nature lifts us out of linear means-end reasoning and helps us to slow down into the pure present, where we can hear God's calming messages or answers to our daily woes. In nature, we can easily experience awe, an emotion so powerful that it humbles us.

What is it about nature that can bring us to such deep inner peace—and sometimes even to our knees?

Mysticism Meets Physics

Great spiritual minds from almost every tradition assert that there is a "Ground of Being" beneath the visible surface of reality as we know it. Judaism, Christianity, and Islam—the three monotheistic religions—are replete with mystical writers and creation mythologies that support the idea of an Original Mind before all Matter. With the help of physics, the postmodern soul is returning to this view of unlimited intelligence, creativity, and pure love energy. It is rediscovering what the shamans have always known—that adequate meaning cannot be found in sensate materialism. Manmade objects are generally sapped of Pure Unlimited Love energy. Nature, on the other hand, was born of it.

According to the Upanishads and other great religious narratives, there was never nothing. The Ground of Being, or Ultimate Reality, pure Mind, beyond time and place, has always been there. It gave rise to the universe through some epic creative event akin to what we would now call "the big bang." In an explosion from a single point 13.7 billion years ago, like a massive fireball giving rise to all that is, Ultimate Reality became energetically manifested in the form of our universe. After a thousandth of a second, the temperature cooled to 100 billion degrees centigrade, enabling elementary particles such as electrons, protons, and neutrons to form. A minute or two later, the temperature dropped a little more, allowing neutrons and protons to combine to form atomic nuclei. Expansion and cooling continued, and after 700,000 years, simple atoms began to form. Galaxies and the first stars took shape, and planet Earth with its massive oceans came into being. Bacteria, plants, fish, animals, and eventually humans formed as a consequence of this explosion.

As the passage from Genesis states, "let there be light," or according to the Gospel of John, "in the beginning was the Word." The energy from this event imbued all of nature, and this energy still exists as the cosmic background radiation of the universe. This original prime energy is divine, pure unlimited love, and it is the source of *everything* that exists in our universe, including humans. This energy, therefore, connects us to *everything*—including nature.

Hazrat Inayat Khan (1882–1927), a Muslim who was born in India and ventured to the West to found the International Sufi Movement in 1918, wrote: "And the love of God is that which is the purpose of the whole creation: if that were not the purpose, the creation would not have taken place. As the whole creation is from God, then it is of God. If it is of God, then it is a manifestation of love, and the manifestation of God is purposed to realize perfection in love."[117]

This is more or less what spirituality, from its beginnings with the great Hindu Upanishads, is talking about. The nature mystics—or those who see nature as a way to connect with the divine—feel this Source in the winds and the waves. Nature mystics claim to be overwhelmed and transformed by a love that nature pours out—a love that is never ending, constant, pure, unconditional, and even wise.

Yet nature mystics feel more than they know. We do not know much about Ultimate Reality, so humility is in order. John Templeton wrote, "I use the word 'humility' here to mean understanding that God infinitely exceeds anything anyone has ever said of Him, and that He is infinitely beyond human comprehension and understanding."[118]

Beyond Ordinary Experience and Perception

The world we see upon waking and experience during the day is material, stable, and concrete. How can we even begin to consider an Ultimate Reality over our everyday reality? One first step is to focus on the subatomic world, which is beyond ordinary experience and perception. We find particles darting into and out of existence in much less than a small fraction of a second. A gluon (a particle within a nucleus that "glues" things together) is created and annihilated almost simultaneously. A neutron lasts about fifteen minutes, making it the longest-lived particle. An electron can appear in the quantum world like a little particle or wavelike cloud that moves at the speed of light.

The quantum world deals with many unobservable quantities (wave functions). Quantum objects can even be in more than one place at the same time (the wave property of electrons), and they can jump without going through intervening space (quantum jump).

Matter turns out to be fairly bizarre stuff. On a physical level, the universe does not seem immaterial and unstable. Yet, at the quantum level, it seems immaterial. It might be suggested that the Original Mind or Ultimate Reality gave rise to the energies and thermodynamic constants of the universe. Nothing is proven. Quantum physics makes the Infinite Mind more plausible by undermining the materialistic philosophy that is often the basis for ruling out God.

Rationalizing the Source is made even more plausible by the extreme improbability of the random occurrence of an event such as a big bang—through which a universe with energy, time, and space suddenly bursts into being from nothingness—and the equally great improbability of universal constants (not to mention space and time) being generated by no originating intelligence.

I do not assert that modern physics proves the existence of a Supreme or Higher Being. We can agree with theorist and writer Ken Wilber: "According to their general consensus, modern physics neither proves nor disproves, neither supports nor refutes, a mystical-spiritual worldview."[119] But all the great physicists that Wilber discusses—including Heisenberg, Schrödinger, Einstein, De Broglie, Jeans, Planck, Pauli, and Eddington—encouraged the dialogue between physics and spirituality. While none of these men thought that physics perfectly demonstrated God, none of them thought that physics refuted such a worldview. Most believed that the idea of Infinite Mind was reasonable. Wilber pointed out that every one of them became mystics, who wrote eloquently of a cosmic religious feeling that informed their lives and their pursuit of science.

It is immensely exciting that first-rate physicists are guided by science to the idea of an Original Mind lying behind the "beginning" of the universe and its immutable laws. Maybe we will discover that love is indeed the basic force in the spiritual and natural worlds.

LOVE: THE GLUE THAT HOLDS THE UNIVERSE TOGETHER?

Could all of nature actually be constituted by love? Physics, chemistry, and mathematics might someday conceivably substantiate this equation. The distinguished physicist Kenneth W. Ford notes that a gluon, the "glue" particle within a nucleus between a neutron and a proton, only lasts for about a billionth of a billionth of a second. Particles such as pions, muons, and neutrinos pop in and out of existence, and photons break down the distinction between particle and wave.

The incessant creation and annihilation of particles gives one the impression that, at this quantum level, the line between being and non-being is fuzzy. Particles come in and out of existence so quickly that they make the blink of an eye look like years. Matter seems to lack solidity and permanence at its quantum level. It is almost ephemeral.

Where are these particles coming from? The idea of the universe being grounded in an underlying matrix of Unlimited Love might fit in here somehow.

The great Hindu M. K. Gandhi, in his classic work *The Law of Love* (1957), refers to love as "more wonderful than electricity." He writes:

> Scientists tell us that without the presence of the cohesive force amongst the atoms that comprise this globe of ours, it would crumble to pieces and we cease to exist; and even as there is cohesive force in blind matter, so must there be in all things animate; and the name for that cohesive force among animate beings is Love.[120]

Love is more than a social-relational energy for many like Gandhi. It is constantly holding together the universe. Gandhi writes that "love sustains the earth."[121]

Nature Restores Us to Who We Are

Regardless of what science tells us, we know from experience that connecting with aspects of the universe—particularly nature—restores us, which is confirmation enough for many of us. Spirituality, at its best, is participating in a divine energy that brings us back to ourselves. In nature we feel restored by the underlying love and creative energy of the universe, which is so much bigger than us. There is much to be gained from the feeling of smallness before the grandeur of a vast sunset as the stars begin to appear. This is a healthy diminishment from the ego-filled dramas of our lives.

We humans come from the womb of nature and are only able to survive as such. In going back to the sacred gift of nature, we can cling fast to dreams and find hope despite the turbulence and catastrophic tones of the world around us. In such spaces, we can turn to the universe (from the Latin *universum*, literally *uni* (one) and *versus* (turned), or "turned toward the one") and feel in freedom that all things are together as a whole. There is a deep flourishing in this togetherness, a flourishing that has been cast aside by industrial devastation and the loss of reverence for nature that is part of the modern world. Nature is our rightful context for flourishing. In such spaces, our spirits regenerate.

Spending time in nature is not a luxury but a healing necessity. The awesome power of nature is everywhere in nature, evoking wonder. Over the centuries in various cultures, nature has been worshipped for its radiance, from the brilliant colors and textures of fall leaves to the snowy white woods. Within the monotheistic traditions, the actual deification of nature is disallowed. To all the great nature mystics—whether Jewish, Christian, or Muslim—nature is deemed a gift from the loving creativity of the divine Mind, a symbol of the interdependent web of all existence that is a part of, but not to be confused with, the divine.

While we as children of Abraham ought not to worship nature, let us all be excited and awed by it as a hint of divine love for each of us. The chambered nautilus is such a perfect spiraled shell that it has often been cherished—not worshipped—as the perfect lustrous coil of heavenly message filled with divine song when touched to the ear. Nature at its best can be deeply cherished as the great signpost to the pure love beneath the surface of our world. Thus, cherishing nature heals the soul and brings about inner peace.

Our minds and well-being require some naturalistic resetting, as captured symbolically in the ancient poem about a Garden of Eden, a place where one had inner peace and simplicity and from which our ancestors were expelled. The Garden is necessary for inner peace, like a walk in Central Park refreshes those who are otherwise compressed by the intensity of ultra-urban life. When the brain feels ready to implode, or when we are just feeling a bit lost in modern-day America, it is a good time to plant a little flower.

Inner peace can be found by first noticing the sacredness of our souls and then the natural world in its sheer magnificence. This natural world includes our galaxy and all the harmonious mathematical constants and thermodynamic principles that turn many physicists into theists.

THE ATTRACTION OF INNER PEACE

Across spiritual traditions, it is said that people who know inner peace and the kindness that flows from it *are somehow recognized by nature*. Creatures, including our pets, recognize a kind and spiritual "holy" person, like St. Francis of Assisi. Mythically, such people have restored a paradise in which there is the renewed peace and healing of an unbroken relationship with nature, the divine, and with one another in loving kindness.

Forgetting Nature

Despite how much we need nature, much of the industrialized world is deeply forgetful of the Original Mind that constitutes the sacred essence of the universe, the natural world, and our souls. We have fallen away from the proper awareness of the sacred essence that underlies all things and constitutes Ultimate Reality. Advancements in industry and technology over the centuries mean that those of us who live in industrialized societies never need to leave our homes to fetch water; cut wood; grow, gather, or hunt for food; or bathe in lakes and rivers. This never-ending drive for comfort and convenience has taken us far away from our place of fulfillment.

Rachel Carson (1907–1964), perhaps the finest nature writer of the twentieth century, challenged the notion that human beings could or should ever obtain mastery over nature. Her classic book *Silent Spring* (1962) warned of the dangers to all natural systems from pesticides such as DDT, and she seriously doubted the direction of modern science. Though her book is more than sixty years old, it is still relevant today, inspiring environmentalists globally.

Carson was deeply concerned about the future. Most of us are, as we adjust to wildfires, hurricanes, drought, and extreme temperatures becoming the norm. We wonder how bad things can get. Although we as humans have disrupted nature's intelligence, we cannot completely destroy it before destroying ourselves first. We are only one of many species. Nature will survive in one form or another—it doesn't need us. We, however, need nature for everything—food, shelter, warmth. These are the gifts of nature given us by the Source.

The consequences of our deep forgetfulness have been disastrous. We have forgotten both who and whose we are. We forget that nature is a sacred gift, the first and most refreshing revelation of a divine love. We abuse nature, ourselves, and one another. We require much more healing than would be necessary had our awareness not been so diminished. Nature's extreme relevance to our well-being is highlighted when it's taken away.

Nature Deficit Disorder

These days, many of my psychiatrist friends are beginning to speak of "nature deficit disorder," a term coined by Richard Louv in his book *Last Child in the Woods: Saving Our Children from Nature-Deficit Disorder*. The disorder is not yet a scientifically validated condition, but it has real symptoms, including high stress and anxiety, depression, and diminished well-being.

Children and young adults suffer from it when they are locked into computer, video game, and cell phone screens. The average American child now spends about *seven hours per day staring at screens*. There are many examples of young adults who appear to be so entrapped by devices that they never look up to the starry skies or across the vista of an open field. They lack deep connection with the earth or the sea and instead grow up in fields of plastic-covered electronic devices. They may not realize how much they miss the peaceful energy of our blue-green planet because they have never known it.

My favorite documentary filmmaker, Delaney Rusten, MD, a Stanford-trained physician, international speaker, and the creator of the award-winning film *Screenagers,* has helped countless families navigate the often dangerous intergenerational conflicts that arise when screens divide family members through lack of communication. *Screenagers*[122] is a brilliant film probing the vulnerable corners of family life and depicting the messy struggles over social media, video games, and academics in the home as young families navigate our digital world.

Scott D. Sampson's book *How to Raise a Wild Child: The Art and Science of Falling in Love with Nature*[123] distills research on the benefit of a child's connection with nature. He writes about how parents can help kids fall in love with nature and how to create child naturalists in your own backyard. He encourages us to imbue our children with the priceless feelings of awe and wonder before the beauty of nature. If our kids grow up too fast, spending time in nature can slow them down, a suggestion offered by psychologist David Elkind in *The Hurried Child: Growing Up Too Fast Too Soon*.[124]

Fulfillment, health, and flourishing all require some regular exposure to nature, exercise, and to real embodied interactions.

HEALING AT HOPEWELL

Robert tells the story of how he had been sleeping in the fields, homeless and hungry. He had experienced several psychiatric episodes and been hospitalized a few times over the years. Now he had finally agreed, with the help of loyal friends, to try a course of treatment. They recommended Hopewell, and he agreed because he would be immersed in nature.

Hopewell was built on an old Amish farm of 350 acres, about an hour outside of Cleveland. The lush green farm fields felt so open and comforting to him, calling his mind to pass gently through the air and over the hills. There was the chicken coup, the red wooden barn, and the Hopewell country store where Amish buggies would pull up and women in their bonnets would come inside to restock the cheese and help out with sales for the day. Cows grazed under feathery clouds both white and hopeful. This all drew Robert in. He worked with various help crews bringing in the eggs, planting the garden, combing the horses, milking the cows, and doing music and art therapy. This all felt free and natural as the Hopewell values of community and positive psychology soaked into his consciousness. He was giving and glowing, and healing with kindness. He became attached to the environment around him. His primary clinician was compassionate and trustworthy. He had a deeply caring doctor who he trusted, and began reshaping his mindset about treatment.

With the small reflection circles speaking of themes such as kindness, forgiveness, gratitude, wisdom, hope, and awe as experienced at Hopewell, Robert no longer missed the cell phones and computers that were absent from his new environment. He stabilized after a few months with light medication and moved closer to nature when he left the facility, moving into a nonprofit that helps people residing in the community. He then found a meaningful job and he found the resilience to receive real help through nature, community, compassion, kindness, and contributing to the lives of those around him. Sure, he still had some healing to do, but thanks to everyone at Hopewell, he felt inner peace.

Reuniting with Nature: The New Science of Awe

One concrete way to experience Ultimate Reality in nature is through awe. Awe is an emotion that flows from the experience of wonder before a fabulous mountain view, when gazing about a vast and ornate cathedral, or when sensing the beauty of another human being through their actions of kindness. It is triggered by an awareness of something vast and beautiful, like when walking into a deep forest and being quietly overwhelmed by its majesty. Awe is a sublime emotion, a feeling of wonder, astonishment, and reverence. It is associated with attitudes of respect, admiration, fascination, exultation, calmness, and even a touch of fear.

Such moments of awe have been the subject of almost every great theologian and philosopher, none greater than Rudolf Otto in his magnificent description of the "mysterium tremendum," where he states that most of spiritual experience is grounded in wonder before the felt presence of "something greater" and "wholly other."

Awe is one of the most powerful positive emotions in terms of its ability to heal. Several decades ago, the brilliant researcher and psychologist Dacher Keltner submitted a grant to the John Templeton Foundation to make awe the center of his research at the University of California, Berkeley. I recommended funding and eventually attended the earliest research meeting at Berkeley as this field started to unfold under Keltner's leadership. Over the years, Keltner's research has revealed the beneficial effects of awe on our mental, emotional, and physical well-being.

Awe, he demonstrates:

- Reduces stress.
- Frees us from self-criticism and encourages self-forgiveness.
- Inspires altruism.
- Allows us to put our anxieties in perspective, contributing to inner peace.
- Frees us from focus on the self and shifts us toward concern for others.

According to Keltner, *awe is one of the most important positive emotions, and it benefits us in numerous ways, including enhanced feelings of well-being, generosity, and humility.*[125] In 2022, Keltner's group published one of their many excellent studies on how older adults can experience social disconnection, anxiety, and sadness, all of which adversely affect aging and health. Those who took fifteen-minute "awe walks"—strolls during which participants gave mindful attention to nature—did better on psychological surveys for mental health and positive emotions such as compassion and gratitude.[126]

When people pause from their busy daily lives and look out at an awesome scene in nature, they often report a sense of transcendence, majesty, and Ultimate Reality. Rudolf Otto observed in his classic work *The Idea of the Holy* (1926) that all deep spiritual experiences are numinous.[127] "Numinous" comes from the Latin word *numen*, which means "divine will." It is also used in conjunction with *luminous*, Latin for "full of light." People often speak of sensing a numinous energy in certain landscapes, such as around Sedona in Arizona. I often visit a spot where the Appalachian Trail cuts through the Delaware Water Gap off Route 80 in Pennsylvania for spiritual uplift. I have a special walking stick carved by an old African American mystic in Cleveland. When he sold it to me, he said, "Follow this stick. It will know more about where you are going than you do."

We use the word "numen" to refer to the feeling of a spiritual influence, force, and energy. The great Canadian artist Emily Carr (d. 1945) spoke of the numinous atmosphere of the forest[128] along the Vancouver coast, with the deep greens and browns of its huge trees, the rocks, and the Pacific waves pounding. Nature is not just something to be analyzed scientifically; it appeals to the *numinous* emotions and feels holy or filled with the mystery of *numinous* presence.

Nature is a door to the spirit behind and within the universe, and awe takes us through the door. These perennial truths have been made current by science. Awe can be overwhelming and powerful enough to set us free from destructive emotions such as bitterness and hostility that sometimes grab our inner being with such force and seem ascendant in our culture. Awe helps untangle us, despite what is going on in the world around us. Being awestruck by the sounds and colors of nature without distraction is a vitamin pill for the soul and an especially important one in an era of such intense political division in the United States. Before nature, acrimony fades.

> ### THE A.W.E. METHOD
>
> Those of us who live in crowded urban areas and industrial centers, those who have little time to spare for awe walks, or those who are physically unable to spend time in nature can still experience the benefits of awe every day. In *The Power of Awe*, lifelong meditators and mindfulness teachers Michael Amster, MD, and Jake Eagle share a brief practice anyone can do at any time to access the healing emotion of awe on a moment's notice, even when far removed from nature, such as while sitting in a sterile office, a nursing home, or in heavy traffic. Their A.W.E. Method stands for Attention, Wait, Exhale and Expand, and the practice, supported by research at UC Berkeley, is clinically proven to reduce depression, anxiety, chronic pain, and burnout while improving overall well-being. For example, you might focus on the movement of branches in the breeze or feeling a pet's fur. In this brief period of close attentiveness, the mind grows peaceful. We do not usually think of these sorts of things as therapeutic, but if we notice them with wonder and awe they become so.

STEWARDSHIP: CARING FOR THE DIVINE

Myths across traditions portray the authority of the saints over the natural world as always one of pastoral care rather than of domination or manipulation. They are in harmony with nature and respond with gentleness to all creatures. The violence of the world does not intrude, and humility abounds in a peaceful affinity and delight.

Our human dependence on nature and our interdependence with creation are underlined, and in this is true dominion, defined as the calling to take loving responsibility for the natural world. This tradition of stewardship love for nature is central to medieval theology and philosophy.

Nature and humans have their own great dignity, as expressions of a higher divine love, and therefore we can find ways to let nature be alongside us. Let us relearn how to cherish the gift of nature and human nature and seek to care for it rather than transpose it. Let us focus human progress on learning to raise kind children, on enjoying the experience of giving and glow, on healing with kindness, on following our Callings, on reconnecting with inner peace, and on cultivating meaning in communities of virtue and character. As for medicine, let us win Nobel Prizes by pursuing therapeutic goals to overcome disease and illness, rather than trying to reinvent the very nature of human nature in a vast dehumanizing genetic endeavor.

The Artists of Nature

I believe that there is an Eternal Artist at work in the universe in Pure Love. This deep creative presence pervades the universe and every soul, creating a wonderful resonance between nature and our inner being. It is no wonder that we feel so comfortable mediating and praying in nature, the greatest cathedral of them all.

Artists who tap into the Source are capable of capturing nature's numinous qualities in a painting or a photograph and can even inspire awe through their work. This was well demonstrated by the various Hudson River painters in the mid-nineteenth century, who painted while on trips into the Catskills and Adirondacks, silently capturing the tremendous mountain cliffs and infinite woods. Some artists in the Hudson River School painted the ocean coasts as well.

The huge popularity of these painters, such as Thomas Cole, brought peace to the souls of Americans in the difficult times that gave rise to Civil War. Cole is generally acknowledged as the founder of the Hudson River School, which includes Frederic Edwin Church with his iconic *Niagara Falls* and Albert Bierstadt with his paintings of the Sierras. This was a way for people to turn their backs for a moment on mundane labors and the modern world and get in touch with a higher Being. Art enabled them to experience the world as both concrete and numinous.

Great artists capture an ego-free unification with nature and cosmos. Jackson Pollock painted in a state of transformed consciousness that would come upon him in his studio. Van Gogh clearly saw the mystical energy in flowers and starry evening skies, so much so that people questioned his sanity. Nature provides a means for the soul to dive deep into the mysterious energy that underlies the universe and rise again to the surface feeling more whole. The magnificent energy alive in nature points to an Ultimate Reality and is a window into the divine. Nature mystics experience the natural world as alive and teeming with divine energy.

Emily Carr, mentioned earlier, was a Canadian postimpressionist artist who painted the Pacific coastal forests—complete with their tremendous deep brown and green sequoias towering above the ground and reaching as high as the eye can see. She was inspired by the spirituality of the indigenous people of the Pacific Northwest Coast. She followed the First Nations, who carved and painted their totems with a powerful feeling for the tremendous elusive energy that lies in these forests. Her images seem radiant and illuminated from within, much like the stained-glass windows of a magnificent cathedral. Her powerful brush strokes seem to make nature flow with a literal life force.

Georgia O'Keefe painted enlarged flowers inspired by New Mexican landscapes. She felt the divine energy in the American desert. She was a deeply mystical artist who sensed a Source in the luminous beauty of the roses that bloom there. She painted the sacredness of nature in a subdued fashion.

Both Carr and O'Keefe could capture the infinity of a flower or tree. They knew that we experience quiet Oneness with divine energy when we are carefully listening to nature. They were awakened to the gift of nature.

Nature's Calling

When people are asked to describe "heaven on earth," they usually include some beautiful natural setting, often garden-like. Nature is a window into a divine mysterious creative energy. Large numbers of people today claim to sense the sacred energy of nature and are attracted to the naturalism that has sustained indigenous cultures from the dawn of human history. We need to do much more to connect ourselves with the universe and nature if we are to be healed and healthy in this relentlessly industrialized and digitized world. How else can we be freed from what the poet W. H. Auden called "the age of anxiety," as technology takes over our lives and severs our minds from nature's awesomeness and its healing energy?[129]

We are called to awaken in love to the gift of nature. The beauty of nature is the first respite when we need to be uplifted from the cares of life. We embark on spiritual retreats to again feel the sacredness of our souls, as amplified by the glory of the natural world. When I was a young boy, we worshipped in a school that was so beautifully in tune with nature that it was always possible to feel joy and to pray as the prayer book suggested:

> O God, we thank you for this universe, our great home; for its vastness and richness, and for the diversity of life of which we are part. We praise you for the arching sky and the blessed winds,

for the driving clouds and the constellations on high. We praise you for the sea and the running water, for the everlasting hills, for the trees, and for the grass under our feet. We thank you for our senses by which we see the splendor of the morning, hear the jubilant songs of love, and smell the breath of spring. Grant us, we pray, a heart wide open to all this joy and beauty, and save our souls from being so steeped in care or so darkened by passion that we pass heedless and unseeing when even the thorn bush by the wayside is aflame with the glory of God.[130]

How Cherishing Nature Heals

What does "cherish" mean in the blessing "May you cherish the Spirit of Nature"? It comes from the Latin *carus*, meaning "beloved," "dear," and "to treat with affection." To cherish the Spirit of Nature is to treat nature with tenderness and affection, cultivate it with care, hold it dear, and love it as a source of meaning and sacredness. To cherish is to appreciate, treasure, value, and dignify.

Khalil Gibran wrote, "Solitude is a silent storm that breaks down all our dead branches."[131] Solitude allows us to pause and let nature wrap itself around us and communicate with us through the sounds of a waterfall, the rustling of leaves, or the songs of early morning birds.

John Muir (1838–1914), the modern mystic-prophet of ecological consciousness, wrote about his insights into nature as a divine gift that is to be cherished. In 1903, he and President Theodore Roosevelt spent three days camping at Yosemite. Deeply inspired, Roosevelt went on to establish the great national parks, reserves, and national forests.[132] Both believed that there is a profound love of nature deep within the human soul, and its expression is part of our intended flourishing.

The celebration of nature stems from an overwhelming emotion of awe at its tremendous mystery in depth, color, form, and beauty. Walt Whitman celebrated a single blade of grass: "I believe a leaf of grass is no less than the journey-work of the stars."[133] From the dawn of human history, people in all places have celebrated nature through rituals, songs, drumming, art, flute, poetry, and dance. Many celebrate nature as a gift from which we can draw healing energies and discover curative herbs. Some people lean against massive tree trunks to feel the flow of healing energy. Every Shaman healer practices healing in and with nature. The energy of Pure Unlimited Love lies behind the majesty of nature at a mystical level.

Our connection with nature does not have to fade over the course of a lifetime. Muir writes, "As age comes on, one source of enjoyment after another is closed, but nature's sources never fail."[134] We can cherish nature from childhood to old age. Lisa Miller's book *The Spiritual Child* presents her research on children and teens who describe themselves as spiritual and experience nature as enchanted. Adults may inhibit these natural sensibilities in the child, trying to move them away from their natural state of being to fit into the task-filled world of doing. The world of chronological time has us rushing to get things done; nature moves us from doing to simply Being.

Gateways to the Divine: Simple Ways to Heal in Nature

Cherishing nature doesn't have to be complicated or involve expensive airline tickets to remote locations. A simple spiritual practice such as gardening can serve as a getaway to the divine and a way of finding inner peace. As our hands work the soil and clear the weeds, we become one with the nurturing, life-sustaining gifts a garden offers in the form of sustenance. By mindfully tending a garden, we become cocreators of these gifts. Gardening is a wonderful way to experience mindfulness—to clear the mind of cluttering thoughts and anxious worries by quietly focusing on the present. Social horticulture, a therapeutic practice centered on gardening, is known to help people suffering with PTSD, loneliness (unwanted solitude), drug or alcohol addictions, pain, and uncontrolled anger and hostility. Many studies show that nature can combat obesity and improve academic performance.

Spending time in nature generally reduces stress, encourages relaxation, and of course stimulates walking. For those like me who do not especially like the atmosphere or close quarters of a sweaty gymnasium, nature walks up a mountain path, along the shore, or in a park setting are essential to cardiovascular health and reduce the risk of high blood pressure.

A simple walk in nature heals the soul. John Muir wrote of autumn leaves, "Climb the mountains and get their good tidings. Nature's peace will flow into you as sunshine flows into trees. The winds will blow their own freshness into you, and the storms their energy, while cares will drop off like the autumn leaves."[135] A daily walk, whether in an urban park, a desert, or a wooded trail has the power to clear and reset a troubled mind.

Try going "off the grid" for an hour, a day, or more. Follow the flow of quiet water or a peaceful breeze. Be silent and feel how mysterious and awesome nature is.

"Forest bathing," a practice popularized in the early 1980s in Japan, is similar to an awe walk in the forest. There is now a lot of good science on forest therapy helping with stress management for all age groups. If you can't shake a grudge, take an hour out in an inspiring park or woods and focus on your breathing; breathe in peace and breathe out hostility. Trained ecotherapists, or those who heal others using nature as therapy, tell us to bathe in nature every day for at least thirty minutes. In this silence, you can listen to nature for answers.

Ecotherapy, also known as nature therapy, is an umbrella term for therapy programs and guided nature-based activities intended to improve mental health. People engage in gardening, wilderness therapy, sailing, and animal-assisted therapy. Studies shows that within limits, ecotherapy can improve self-control, self-esteem, social and emotional skills, and even employability.

I grew up in a sailing family and recall how when we were out on the water moving with the wind and the waves, we were less likely to argue. Sailing in calmer winds is mesmerizing and, even in heavier winds, it requires full concentration on managing sails and rigging. Out on the water, under sail with no engine running, we have to relinquish control to the natural winds and tides.

The best book on ecotherapy might be *Ecotherapy: Healing with Nature and Mind*, edited by Linda Buzzell and Craig Chalquist. This book is built on work published decades ago by the Sierra Club in the groundbreaking anthology *Ecopsychology: Restoring the Earth, Healing the Mind*. This booming field assumes rightly that people are inseparable from the rest of nature and thereby are nurtured by healthy interactions with nature. Research also suggests that childhood experience in nature contributes to creativity and curiosity.

Physicians in the social prescribing movement in the National Health Service in the UK, in Canada, and about thirty countries total do "prescribe nature," in addition to volunteerism. Thus, we begin to see something akin to the Hopewell model in general primary care systems. This is captured well in the 2024 book *Social Prescribing*. South Korea has a nature therapy program for firefighters and others with PTSD, and in Finland mainstream psychiatry prescribes five hours a month in nature to reduce depression and alcoholism through the Flow With Nature (FWN) program, which is thriving in five cities as an accepted rehabilitation treatment. Patients meet in parks, urban and rural forests, by the water, with each meeting lasing about 1.5 hours. Participants meditate, reflect on positive psychological topics, and do yoga-like exercises. The outcomes are hopeful and impressive.

Many young people these days want to reconnect with nature and to cherish it anew. No longer willing to cater to the autonomous technology that forces them to step into a matrix, they prefer to quit work and join global eco-village networks to practice regenerative agriculture and ecotherapy. They choose to live in the cultural context of indigenous eco-spirituality. Around the world, young people are forming eco-spiritual communities for survival and regeneration, as the urban centers of industrial civilization expand and remove us from the beauty, wonder, and spirit of the universe.

My work since the early 1990s has focused on people with dementia, or as I prefer, "deeply forgetful people," and includes helping to initiate animal therapy with well-trained manageable dogs like Labrador Retrievers. Dogs 4 Dementia is the first time in Australia that expert Dementia Centre consultants have partnered up with skilled Assistance Dogs Australia trainers to place dogs into the homes of people living with dementia. A dog is carefully chosen to match household personalities and trained to meet their specific needs. Dementia service dogs are now in fourteen nations. Here is a little email I received from someone who attended a workshop I delivered in Brooklyn Heights on dementia guide dogs some years ago:

> Bringing Lola to see Alzheimer patients has made a tremendous difference in helping me open up the line of communication. Take Marvin, who is ninety-one and lives at home with his wife.

He has advanced Alzheimer's disease. He has a full-time aide and sleeps in his own room while his wife has the master bedroom. Marvin had walked into her bedroom and fell asleep in the bed since the morning.... The aide and his wife couldn't get him up. I walked in the room with Lola, put her paws up on him, and said, "Marvin get up, look who came to visit." Marvin popped up excited to see Lola. I was able to lure him out of bed and into the family room where his wife was. He couldn't contain his excitement. His wife and the aide couldn't believe it. Lola brought back his memory of his dog Sparky![136]

Tips for Cherishing Nature

- Go on nature walks and take your kids if you have any.
- Give children nature experiences that allow for real connection.
- Do some gardening and watch things grow.
- Meditate in a natural setting and breathe in the divine energy.
- Add plants to the workplace as well as lush green images of nature.
- Add plants and dogs to assisted living centers or nursing homes.
- Encourage your hospital to build nature into the hospital environment, which all the best places are doing nowadays, because it improves resilience and speeds up recovery by reducing stress hormones.
- Have your kids look after a pet. It is one of the best things for their sense of responsibility for nature and for other human beings.
- Chant. For most Hindus, Buddhists, Sikhs, and Jains, the intonation *Om* is a sacred vibration that centers the mind on the Source, or Brahman. By chanting *Om* during meditation,

we attune our inner selves with the cosmic Mind and its prime energy.

My Nature Meditation

As I take the ferry across the Long Island Sound from Port Jefferson, I meditate before the vast beauty of the ocean waves. After a busy day at work, I do nothing other than be inspired by the universe and its astonishing energies as a contrast with my fleeting smallness. On rare occasions, I take the car onto the ferry and get off at Bridgeport in Connecticut to drive up to the Yale Peabody Museum in New Haven, where I can experience awe while standing quietly before a great work of art, or perhaps listening to a Bach concert over at the Divinity School. I'm not in nature here, but I am in awe.

Find a place in nature that is quiet and inspiring and sit comfortably for a few minutes as you breathe deeply in through your nose and exhale through your mouth. Build this practice into your day as best you can. Relax your body from forehead to feet. Let emotions drift away. Breathe more slowly. Close your eyes and enter your own inner stillness. Feel inward peace by connecting with the tranquil sounds of nature around you. Let the music of nature fill your awareness. Notice the movement of the air and the breeze and feel the colorful energies of nature.

The Wheel of Love in Cherishing the Gift of Nature

The Way of Helping

In many instances, those who self-report the "helper's high" will have been raking leaves in the park or around the school grounds or cleaning up the beach. This combination of helping others and being immersed in nature is especially effective in moving us to inner peace.

If you see a turtle on the road, stop carefully and give it a lift to a nearby lake. Notice that in nature there are so many magnificent examples of one creature helping another. Darwin wrote about group altruism, about the immense advantage that the evolution of kindness and altruism benefits the group in which it evolves.

The Way of Creativity

Nature is nothing if not pure creativity following the seasons. As part of nature, our human creativity is generally closely linked to love. Much of human creativity is driven or shaped by the dynamic of love, whether in the family, between friends, in the neighborhood, at work, or for all humanity. Many wonderful musical compositions are dedicated to a particular loved one—such as Bach's pieces for his daughter Anna.

Concluding Thoughts

Nature is a gift, one given by the divine as an expression of infinite love. Though the Maker of this universe for many is Ultimate Reality, its love is expressed through the natural world, and so nature is love's great Gift. No wonder Jesus often went out to the hills to find peace and quiet.

It is impossible to consider inner peace without considering love of nature. The nature mystics of all indigenous traditions see nature as the expression of the same original One Mind energy. They have an overwhelming feeling of a cherishing divine love that lies behind the beauty of the green grass and the blue sky, the sublime refreshment of the newly fallen pure white snow, or the blooming flowers of spring.

We escape to nature to experience a healthy renewed feeling of awe. We must turn off the TV, set aside the screens, step out of the virtual reality of technology, and escape to the beauty of the natural world to find well-being, security, and inner peace.

CHAPTER 7

The Seventh Path: May You Honor the Spirit of Freedom

> "Now the Lord is the Spirit, and where the Spirit of the Lord is, there is freedom."
>
> —2 Corinthians 3:17
>
> "Life without liberty is like a body without a spirit."
>
> —Khalil Gibran
>
> "Freedom and love go together."
>
> —Jiddu Krishnamurti

"Freedom" is a common word, and one that many of us don't give much thought to. As adults in the free world, we choose what to wear, where to work, what color car to buy, where to hang our hat. We decide what we're hungry for, how much we'll eat, and whether we'll cook or dine out. And we decide whether to belong to a church, synagogue, or mosque and who to vote for. There's freedom of choice, freedom of speech, freedom of religion, freedom of will, freedom to abide by the law or break it. These are *external freedoms* that are exercised by being unfettered and unrestricted.

External freedom is a matter of having the social space and liberty to act on our thoughts and self-chosen purposes. External freedom can also mean something much more consequential, such as freedom from the power of another. When we don't have freedom, we often will show great courage in regaining it. With freedom comes responsibility to preserve it. It is in this sense a duty.

Where, though, does this blessed urge for freedom come from? What lies beneath the perennial human quest for freedom? Freedom ultimately has its origins in the One Mind, our spiritual inner being. I refer to this as "internal freedom," or an energy of spirit or soul.

Creativity: The Mystery of Internal Freedom

It's easy to comprehend and define external freedoms, but the internal freedom that drives us is more elusive. Internal freedom lives on a spiritual level. Internal freedom is an aspect of the original One Mind that lies within each of us. When we yearn to follow a calling, create a piece of art, or to change the course we've taken in life, we are feeling internal freedom—the freedom to cocreate with God. In a very real sense, this is the ultimate pathway, for exercising internal freedom requires a spiritual connection with the One Mind that can only be achieved by following the other six pathways in this book.

For some, acting on or following the call of internal freedom means fighting for a cause, for others it means giving up a successful career to care for a loved one, for others it means writing a screenplay or painting a canvas. When we act on this spiritual drive, we honor and acknowledge the divine spark within ourselves. The relevance of this internal, self-guiding drive is much greater than many of us realize. How and whether we respond to this call to cocreate determines as major aspect of inner peace.

The great Silver Age Russian philosopher Nikolai Berdyaev (1874–1948) believed that the dawn of the twentieth century would bring an end to materialism and slavery in a new era of spirituality and love in freedom. In this heaven on earth, we would all tap into the divine creative powers of our true consciousness, collaborating with the divine in continuing the cocreation of the world. He wrote that "God so loved freedom that he allowed his own Son to be crucified, for truth nailed upon a cross compels no one other than by the attractive power of love."[137]

Berdyaev saw creativity in all its positive forms as part of the mystery of freedom. He also wrote that freedom is "the power to create out of nothing, the power of the spirit to create out of itself." He wrote in metaphysical terms of our becoming fully aware of the human self as a free and spiritual being.

Internal and external freedoms are essential to any flourishing human being. Ideally, we have both simultaneously. Internal freedom is self-guiding, so it can exist without external freedom; external freedom is freedom to pursue these self-guided callings unfettered by the restricting powers that be.

People need internal freedom to feel whole and external freedom to pursue their dreams. External freedom without an inner compass (inner freedom centered on love), however, leads to abuse of freedom. When self-guided by internal freedom, we are always on the right track.

The freedom to think, dream, create, and love lies within each of us. Although it can be dampened by forced servitude, financial constraints, or disapproval, it cannot be hindered entirely by these types of external forces. Internal freedom can survive external constraint—think of people like Dietrich Bonhoeffer, Martin Luther King Jr., and Nelson Mandela.

Free Minds and Free Spirits

We described the original One Mind in chapter 5. But what aspect of the One Mind involves freedom? The great Nobel Prize–winning Austrian physicist Erwin Schrödinger (1887–1961), the father of quantum physics who was enough of a genius to actually prove Einstein's theory of relativity, wrote, "The total number of minds in the universe is one. In fact, consciousness is a singularity phasing within all beings."[138] This is one of the most famous statement of twentieth-century science. He argued that multiplicity of minds is illusion, as there is only one single original free consciousness that expresses itself in many ways, and that cannot be accounted for in physical terms or in terms of anything else. *Consciousness, by definition, is inherently free to express itself in many ways*, and "consciousness cannot be accounted for in physical terms."[139] Freedom, then, comes with the gift of the mind. Human freedom is divine freedom within otherwise earthen beings.

Human beings are free spirits, or they are otherwise nothing but predetermined collections of molecules. There is a debate as to whether we are human beings having spiritual experiences or spiritual beings having a human experience. Sir John Eccles, Nobel laureate for his work on communication between brain cells. viewed the individual mind as part of a larger One Mind, which is in and of itself free. There was also Karl Jung, with his Collective Unconscious, in which at the deepest level of mind we are all interconnected and one. Thus he could write about synchronicity, or events in which we realize this profound connectivity of Mind. No one has ever disproven the existence of an eternally free soul, which looks more plausible than ever. We cannot claim to be full-blown materialists and at the same time assert a nonmaterial aspect of our being. Mind and Soul are synonymous.

To be a free center of creativity and love within the infinite field of One Mind means that the human represents a spiritual break from the determinations of nature. We are above nature when we burst weightlessly into a freedom that is, by its very essence, eternal and spiritual, rather than material. Look up to the limitless sky when thinking about freedom, rather than downward into the ground. The logs burning in a fireplace will simply turn to dust; above them, the shooting flowing flames are free and unconstrained.

The mystics understand this easily: Freedom is a spiritual gift and represents the very essence of the divine Mind within each of us, the awareness of which brings inner peace. Therefore, we must honor and dignify it. It does not originate in the state, and the state must control the tendency to repress freedom. The freedom of the spirit is higher than the state. St. Paul wrote (I Corinthians 7:23), "You were bought at a price; do not become slaves to human beings."[140] Freedom is a calling, and we are responsible to the Supreme Being to cherish and respect it in ourselves and others as a matter of duty.

When Internal and External Freedom Are at Odds

Sometimes, the spiritual gift of freedom becomes opaque, repressed by various temptations that elevate the material over the spiritual. Pure freedom requires us to understand it as a gift from the Supreme in which it has its origin. It is this higher spirit of freedom to which honor is due.

Freedom is resilient, like the blooming lotus that rises in the early morning sunlight from the dark muddy waters in which it sits. It is a fully resilient inner spiritual reality, and it eventually rises up from the ground of our souls like a phoenix, affecting the structure of society. That immortal bird in Greek mythology was always reborn from the ashes of its immediate predecessor. It can be said that over the course of history outer organizational freedom has tended to rise above its undertakers because it is part of the very nature of the original Mind that lies within every person. Even the great Genghis Khan (d. 1227), founder of the Mongol Empire, insisted that people be free to believe whatever they want to and that at least no women be kidnapped and taken into slavery.

When freedom lacks internal self-control, eventually the tyrants take over and freedom is diminished for a while even as it is also being reborn from the spirit with new champions. In *The Wasteland* (1922), T. S. Eliot depicts a world of brokenness and loss in the wake of the First World War. The great poet conjures an image of barbarity being rudely forced on all, and where anything consistent with truth, goodness, and beauty is detested. This is the downward vortex of mere materialism.

Ruthless regimes do their best to restrict external and internal freedom. How many great disciples of love have prayed that heavy shackles be removed from their wrists and ankles? How many great leaders have been imprisoned when they wrote their most influential books? These would include the Reverend Martin Luther King Jr. with his *Letters from a Birmingham Jail*, Dietrich Bonhoeffer's *Letter and Papers from Prison*, St. Paul, who wrote most of his letters in Roman prisons, and countless others over the centuries. So many exemplars of pure love have been imprisoned unjustly because they were called to speak truth to power. Despite external confinement, they were still driven to restore love and freedom in the outer world through the power of the pen.

FREEDOM FROM SELF-DESTRUCTIVE BEHAVIORS

For many people, unhealthy behaviors such as smoking, overeating, or angering easily are coping mechanisms—ways to deal with stress or to escape uncomfortable feelings, whatever they may be. Letting them go is a choice, but it's not usually an easy one. Respecting another's autonomy is the only successful approach in working with people who freely desire to improve their lives by changing an unhealthy behavior. Freedom and love are always found together in any successful effort to help anyone turn their life around for the better.

Working in a department of preventive medicine, I am surrounded by experts in helping patients change their unhealthy behaviors. They all begin by asking if the one in need realizes that change is a good idea and necessary. Patients may still have to, as the expression goes, "bottom out" before change is possible. Like anyone associated with a department of preventive medicine, I have learned how to nurture this change:

- Ask a person if they really want to change.
- Ask the person how they would like to get started.
- Invite the person to write their first step down in a simple sentence on paper because this has been proven to deepen their commitment.
- Plan and schedule a follow-up meeting first to discuss progress and then to reflect on obstacles that might have arisen and call for an adjustment.
- Always demonstrate empathy and concern, but never get judgmental or threatening because carefrontation is creative.
- Respect them as autonomous agents.

In our more than twenty peer-reviewed articles (combining researchers from Case Western, Harvard, and Stony Brook) on 12-Step recovery programs, mainly looking at Alcoholics Anonymous and Narcotics Anonymous, there is no success in recovery without love and freedom.

Love, Creativity, Freedom, and Justice

For thinkers and activists across a wide range of contexts and historical experiences, unconditional love, spiritual experience, and the rigorous pursuit of justice in the world constitute a powerful path to social transformation, as they always have, but only when they are strongly linked together. "Spiritual activists" draw on spiritual worldviews and practices to sustain an inner equilibrium of compassion and well-being while continually engaged at the hard edges of social change. They practice what has come to be termed "engaged spirituality" of freedom, love, and justice.

Some spiritual practitioners cast the world aside in favor of a socially disengaged serenity. Of course, there are many great exemplars of love who practice compassionate care with patients in the hospital and that is what they feel called to do. But others are called to take on the difficult work of organizing the downtrodden into groups capable of exerting social and political pressure through persuasion and protest and do so with reliance on a background picture of a universe in which love and justice go with, rather than against, the grain of the Universe.

Spirituality in activism is not new, but it is too often ignored by those who do not see it as a driving dynamic. Yet many of the great social activists, from early antislavery Quakers to the those involved in the civil rights movement, were spiritual activists within a monotheistic framework. The prophetic tradition of Judaism exhorts, "and what does the Lord require of you but to do justice, and to love kindness, and to walk humbly with your God."[141] Perhaps we think of the classical Christian saint, in the style of a St. Francis, as far too removed from the world to be interested in organizing the victims of ensconced group selfishness in order to establish a fairer balance of power through social and political suasion and coercion. But a pure love ethic does not ignore the acrimonious fray of the competing claims of classes, races, and nations, where rough solutions have to be achieved. This is the hard work of love that does justice.

> ### WHY LOVE DOES JUSTICE
>
> Consider the following story from Jim LaRue, a campus chaplain turned housing advocate who has worked in Cleveland neighborhoods for many years:
>
> There are millions who have had a "memorable moment" with Dr. King. Mine became a "formative moment" and occurred while a student at Bucknell University in the late 1950s.
>
> I was one of the student leaders who participated in a chapel service at which Dr. King spoke. But my formative moments came during a lengthy lunch with Dr. King, the other students on the platform that day, and several faculty. Having come from a small southeastern Pennsylvania town, I had no experience that would allow me to fully appreciate what was happening to him as the civil rights struggle he was leading started finding its way into the headlines of newspapers in the North. During our lunch he shared his great fear that his nonviolent approach would be met with such violence that his followers might feel they must finally retaliate with violence.
>
> But he said he was firmly convinced that only love could change the way the game of racism was played. My formative moment came when he described the difference between love as expressed in personal acts of kindness and love expressed through social justice, and that one assumes the other. He said we cannot genuinely have one without the other. Helping someone in need fix their shelter can be a personal act of kindness, but if we do not address the poverty that created the conditions forced upon this person, we are not facing the whole truth.[142]

How does the spiritual activist refuse to hate the people who perpetuate injustice? How can an underlying love of all allow the activist to cope with adversity? How does the spiritual activist maintain a "higher self"? The answer is that they cultivate love, courage, and hope through spiritual practice in the face of indifference and weariness. Spiritual practice provides the activist with the resilience and energy to stick with Pure Unlimited Love, even when confronting serious resistance in challenging aspects of injustice.

Honoring Love, Creativity, and Freedom

In 2015 I was in Bangalore, India, speaking on freedom and consciousness at the Institute for Advanced Studies of Consciousness, where Hindu scientists and philosophers consider the human qualities of love, creativity, and freedom. The Hindus see these strengths as emanating from the Supreme or Original Mind, some small part of which constitutes each individual consciousness. As the Hindus have written, the Supreme is beyond time and place and holds within it the qualities of pure love, creativity, and freedom. *Our human purpose is to honor these gifts so that we may manifest these three great qualities, which bring inner peace.*

There is no love or creativity without the spirit of freedom. These three together define the state of inner peace within the Supreme say the Hindu scriptures. Each human being, by virtue of being a drop of this divine essence, also is born to be free, loving and creative.

It is hard for many people in Western cultures to think of freedom as a high spiritual gift to be honored as sacred. Instead, we tend to think of freedom in terms of economic self-interest or perhaps as a free competition for some commonly desired scarce commodity. But many of the world's populations outside of the modern secularized West do view freedom as gift of the Supreme Being in which we share some spark.

In my own research, fully half of primary caregivers for older adults with dementia believe that their loved ones are "still there" as souls and that their expressions of unexpected fleeting lucidity are signs of their eternal beings.[143] Freedom still resides in the idea that Mind-Spirit precedes Matter and is the primary locus of freedom as it is of Pure Unlimited Love.

The Ayurvedic texts of ancient India state that after the birth of the universe through something like what we today call a Big Bang, the human came into being with the gift of mind (or spirit) and its freedom. In other words, human beings have the potentiality to connect with the Supreme Source since we are of that Source and share in its inalienable creativity, love, and freedom.

Freedom is more than a constitutional right. Freedom is a bright light within the soul that can never be extinguished. Freedom has a source in something beyond and above this world of matter and body. We dishonor the spirit of freedom when we harm and humiliate others or force people to do things that violate themselves in mind, heart, or body. Coercion and constraint, intimidation, repression, and violence threaten freedom and invade our inner peace.

Freedom without such honor cannot last. Many people are anxious about this threat to freedom and equate it with the end of times. But there is a solution. When we take our mind off divisive current events and concentrate on being a kind and helpful neighbor—on following the Seven Pathways—we not only return to the spirit of freedom but keep it alive in those we encounter as well.

There is hope in a nation of freedom-honoring individuals, and it is a great testimony to the human spirit that so many men and women who have been thrown into the prisons of totalitarian nations rise above their constraints to become our greatest champions of freedom.

Freedom and the "American Dream"

In 2015 I was invited to speak in Manhattan at an event where to my surprise serious professors and legal scholars from Yale and Columbia were arguing that we should do away with nations. It was time, they said, to reverse the Peace of Westphalia, a series of treaties signed in 1648 in Europe from which the modern nation-state system was born. The treaties established the principle of Westphalia sovereignty, which states that each nation-state has sovereignty over its own affairs. The treaties ended the age of religious wars across Europe by recognizing the validity of Catholicism, Lutheranism, and Calvinism.

The people at this event did not respond well to my statement that the human psyche needs to live in symbols and particular cultural narratives with which people identify. We human beings need regulated borders and unique cultural identities, for however much we love all humanity, we must still make special commitments to our families, societies, cultures, and nations. To care in a special way for the safety and security of our loved ones, neighbors, and society is the way humans grow up in connection with the narrative of their lives and sources of meaning within the realities of time and place.

While the American dream is often interpreted as an ascent up the ladder of wealth, it is far less about money and possessions than it is about freedom. James Truslow Adams, in *The Epic of America* (1931), coined the term "the American dream." He defined it as "that dream of a land in which life should be better and richer and fuller for every man [person], with opportunity for each according to ability or achievement.... It is not a dream of motor cars and high wages merely, but a dream of a social order in which each man and each woman shall be able to attain to the fullest stature of which they are innately capable, and be recognized by others for what they are, regardless of the fortuitous circumstances of birth or position."[144] There is much truth in these words.

To heal America, we need to make the American dream more complete than ever. The American dream is situated in a Constitutional Republic that includes many democratic elements, but that is not a democracy in any simple sense of the term, and no pure democracy has ever existed. "Republic" here does not refer to a political party. It means *res publica*, or a way of organizing a government that works for the good of all. Article IV of our Constitution reads in part: "The United States shall guarantee to every State in this Union a Republican Form of Government." A republic is not a monarchy, but neither is it a simple democracy. A republic is first and foremost a representative form of government. Our republic is comprised of laws existing within the confines of a constitution. As the US Supreme Court landmark decision of 1803 stated it (*Marbury v. Madison*), "A law repugnant to the Constitution is void."[145] Still, many elements of limited democracy are contained in our republic. When our elected representatives meet to create laws, they debate and they vote. If a bill passes by majority, it then has to be approved by the executive branch.

America is not a perfect example of freedom, nor has any other nation ever reached such heights. The nation had slavery at its founding, which it eventually pushed back through constitutional amendments, a gruesome civil war, public criticism of the KKK, a civil rights movement, and equal opportunity measures. Americans who fought for the end of slavery and freedom for people of color were exercising love, creativity, and freedom—guidance from the Supreme—to acknowledge that souls do not have any color other than the bright radiant light of love.

We see before us in America a neo-Marxist cultural revolution that like all Marxism seeks to destroy by four actions:

1. Divide wherever it can so that national unity and morale are weakened.
2. Undermine the tradition of family, which is the foundation for raising kind children.
3. Destroy the historical narrative and symbols of a nation that provide citizenry with identity.
4. Destroy the spiritual and religious foundations of society.

Freedom in America over the centuries has seen an uneven ascent, and though it has low periods, there is on the whole more respect for individual conscience than ever contemplated in the past. At least freedom is a clear growing aspiration that many Americans have died for. And the regrettable fact of slavery and other restrictions does not negate this remarkable ascent.

The First Amendment

Patrick Henry refused to sign the US Constitution unless a Bill of Rights was added to it. As free beings, we humans pursue truth as best we can through open and free debate in the public square, knowing that we may never get perfectly to the truth, but we can approach it in humility. We seek truth by listening to perspectives that are different from our own to see what we might learn. Freedom of mind and speech are necessary for the evolution of good public policy, building on educational debates in our schools where youth develop skills for argument. The First Amendment to the Constitution is our most precious American political and moral statement of freedom, and it is something to which anyone of any political party pledges allegiance upon assuming a public office, and these solemn words should be taken seriously because they are among the most significant words in all of human history:

> Congress shall make no law respecting an establishment of religion, or prohibiting the free exercise thereof; or abridging the freedom of speech, or of the press; or the right of the people to peaceably assemble, and to petition the government for a redress of grievance.[146]

American healers revere the First Amendment with its affirmation of freedom of spirit and conscience and value a social fabric in which people protect the freedom of their neighbor as much as their own.

Effective education requires freedom of thought and of speech, and without this a free society cannot survive for long. Such freedom seems less welcome in some American schools today than it once was, as far too many students at leading universities and professional schools prefer to shout down an invited distinguished speaker with whom they may disagree than engage in the more intellectually demanding endeavor of open debate. This is like a child putting fingers in their ears while shouting out loudly so as not to hear the words they disagree with.

All true activists invite respectful debate in a process of clarification and, where possible, consensus building. From the time of the early Greeks, open debate has required us to take seriously the very best arguments that an opponent might craft and show that they do not hold up in the court of reason. The last thing we should do is to force silence and censor.

THE FOUR FREEDOMS

Freedom is ultimately more important spiritually than security and it is something for which so many have set aside security and sacrificed their lives. Security can be the enemy of freedom when human beings at times relinquish freedom to please the hand that feeds them. We each have a spiritual urge and a related duty to live freely in a manner that is consistent with our essence. People do not "live by bread alone," spoke Jesus.[147]

"The substance, the essence of spirit . . . is freedom."[148] Hegel's words ring true. "Freedom" is a word to cherish. It comes from the Old English *freo*, meaning "exempt from," with respect to bondage, obstruction, and external restraints. Some have said that just being embodied is a restraint on the spirit. We speak of freedom of mind, religion, speech, belief, and the right to pursue one's callings.

But in a certain sense, security is also necessary for freedom. We need a school curriculum based on Martin Luther King Jr. and on the four freedoms laid out by Franklin Delano Roosevelt in his third State of the Union address in January 1941, eleven months before the United States entered WWII. He wanted to ensure that Americans knew what they were defending. He went beyond the First Amendment freedoms of speech and religion to include "freedom from want" and "freedom from fear." This was novel and immensely valuable at a time when the Depression left so many people penniless and unemployed.

Roosevelt gave Americans jobs building national parks, tunnels, and highways—activities that utilized hard work and developed skill sets for a post–WWII building boom. Two years earlier, Mayor LaGuardia celebrated the four freedoms of speech, worship, press, and assembly at the 1939 New York World's Fair. Roosevelt's four freedoms of 1941 seem to be persuasive and successfully inspired a nation quite reluctant to enter another European war after the horrible losses of American youth in WWI. His declaration still seems to hold true:

Freedom of Speech
Freedom of Worship
Freedom from Want
Freedom from Fear

Today many of us live in fear as the streets of our cities are not well policed, and we are living in want as well. Still, the great Roosevelt placed the First Amendment freedoms of speech and worship before the second two. American families and schools must embrace all four of these freedoms if we are to survive as a free society.

Honoring the Pathways to Freedom

Where and how do we begin to honor freedom? Having read this book, you already hold the key. Following the first Six Pathways frees the spirit in every way.

We honor freedom whenever we Give and Glow, which frees the self from problems of the self. By abiding in the positive version of the Golden Rule, we are so caught up in loving kindness that we use our imagination to consider how we can contribute with our talents to the security and well-being of others. This is liberating in a deep inner sense, but it also empowers a freedom from external coercions.

We honor freedom when we approach every interaction with the intent to heal the people around us, even in casual conversation by our kind words. Small acts of kindness kept me inwardly free in a large medical center during the worst of COVID-19. I found myself cheering people up by listening to them, offering reassuring words, and sometimes with tasteful light mirth if and when the timing felt right. I made a point of being in my office each day so that students could come in and debrief. Some published impressive research papers on how kindness and altruism seemed to uplift them and help them cope with loneliness. But this commitment to kindness is for everyone, everywhere, for them to give and live better.

We honor freedom when we follow our callings and develop our gifts to contribute to the lives of others. Our freedom is violated when we get off course and do things that are not true to our inner being. Continue to cultivate your natural gifts and use them to benefit others even through times of disappointment and rejection, as this is a common fate in every life. Friends who understand you as a person with callings and integrity, and who will help keep you to get back on track instead of straying—these people are your true stars.

We honor freedom when we raise kind children who can make our world a better place and use their freedom for the good. They generally do better in school, avoid antisocial behavior pretty much entirely, stay out of jails, and have more opportunities because few workplaces choose to have unkind people on the team. When kids are free to do good for others, they are spared a great deal of disappointment and failure and are likely to have successful relationships.

We honor freedom when we know the One Mind, which affords us the mindfulness and self-control to understand freedom and inner peace as sacred gifts. Whether taking a few minutes in the early morning to meditate or pray, pausing midday, or looking back over the day in the evening, all are important in the well-formed life. When we do not develop a spiritual practice, we are likely to be caught up in reactivity to the adverse challenges and annoyances of the day. This is not freedom but emotional captivity.

We honor freedom when we cherish nature and enjoy the awesome beauty of the earth, freeing us from anxiety and stress. What could be more inwardly freeing than "forest bathing" or watching the waves come into the beach with their peaceful rhythms. Hence, when we cherish nature we are also practicing our freedom from the pressures and anxieties of the work-a-day world and from the grip of the Internet.

Freedom is essential to all the ways of love in this book, both as a starting assumption and as a product. Simply stated, there can be no love without freedom, and no manifestation of love without freedom.

Exercising Our Freedom

Internal freedom requires inner practice of mindfulness, meditation, prayer, and spiritual beauty, like the lotus—the universal and especially Eastern symbol of spirituality (purity, freedom, love, rebirth, resilience, healing, enlightenment) because it emerges beautiful from the murky water in the morning and is radiant, opening as the sun also rises. We can remain pure in mind and heart regardless of muddy context, rising and blooming above all adversity and darkness.

How do we exercise external freedom? By defying those who would steal our freedom and by setting up social and political structures that allow us to resist those who would abuse power. The power of love has always resisted the love of power, and both aspects are real in the world.

Tips for Honoring the Spirit of Freedom

- Develop a daily spiritual practice that keeps you in tune with your spiritual callings, big and small.
- Act on your spiritual callings, knowing that you will be making a difference. A spiritual calling can be related to work, social justice, caregiving, or simply a kind gesture such as opening a door for another person.
- When you see an injustice, speak up, whether to the parties involved or a trusted source of authority.
- Use your freedom wisely. If you believe you are abusing your freedom, take steps to understand why and get professional help if need be to help overcome addictions or habits that distance you from your free spirit.

My Evening Meditation

I meditate on freedom in the evening with gratitude in my heart. The responsibilities and burdens of the day are over with, and it is time to be reflective about how well I honored the loving spirit of freedom in my encounters over the course of the day. This is the time for an inner retreat into the sanctuary of the One Mind, and in a state of deep relaxation, I imagine the original freedom that all great spiritual traditions envision as an essential aspect of the Supreme Being.

During my several years of evening volunteering as a chaplain in a male prison outside of Cleveland, I met men of all classes and races who were torn away from families and communities for long periods and were sustained only by their unfolding inner faith and the occasional visits by a loved one. Most of them committed serious crimes and imprisonment was reasonable. But many had been spiritually transformed over the years and were peaceful in their minds and hearts.

In fact, we had a spiritual exercise with everyone sitting on chairs in a circle:

1. Breathe deeply and relax your muscles from forehead to toes.
2. Place several fingers on the middle of your forehead and envision your mind as a small point within a much wider field of Mind, receiving loving thoughts.
3. Move those same fingers downward to rest over your chest near your heart and imagine your loving emotions as a small area of love energy within a universal field of love.
4. Feel yourself in a state of peace in mind, heart, and body.

Then we would spend another twenty minutes talking about kindness to be given and received the next day. We would envision encounters around Grafton where loving kindness could be manifested with warmth.

My job was to counsel the prisoners, which really meant being ready to listen with gentle curiosity while they told their life stories. Some of them expressed hope that the power of God would someday deliver them with an unexpected pardon. Often, they spoke of spirit and loving kindness and about how if they could have a second life they would use their freedom for the purpose of love and love alone. After discussions, we would meditate and pray in small groups on the need for more love in the world.

I learned those years ago at the Grafton Correctional Institution that there are people in jail who really don't belong there anymore. These prisoners were profoundly free from bitterness and hatred, hostility and rage. They were now prayerful and so very kind. Some were downright saintly. They were not free to roam the earth as they pleased, but they had found an internal freedom, a spiritual freedom, an inner peace.

We can all every evening focus on a region in the forehead that lies about an inch back behind and between the eyes. This is where we can look into eternity, in the awareness of the soul, moving away from mundane consciousness of matter and the physical senses. There is something beyond perception. Soul consciousness transcends the world of circumstance into a world of light and the presence of the Supreme. As the Brahmas say, we can be aware of the Supreme in the field or dimension of light.

Those who have remembered experiences of death describe a field of bright light and pure unlimited love.[149] When at total peace, it is possible to experience this light and love in daily life, to become free of all else.

This is the light and love in which inner peace exists, and from this comes outward peace. World peace follows from the presence of the divine within us. All is contained within us through this point. People of every culture and experience have shared this image of the divine as light and love. The research on near-death experiences consistently shares the detachment from the body and movement through some tunnel at the end of which they encounter Pure Unlimited Love, an oceanic presence of infinite love and compassion that is perfectly giving and forgiving and truthful no matter what a person's track record.

THE WHEEL OF LOVE AND THE SPIRIT OF FREEDOM

Every spoke on the Wheel of Love is an exercise of freedom— *celebration* to those who need affirmation, *compassion* to those who are suffering, *forgiveness* to those who are burdened by the past and cannot be free without offering an apology if possible, *listening* to those who have been silenced or censored and thus feel invisible, *carefrontation* to keep those we love from veering off course with regard to their deepest values, *helpfulness* to people who could use it, *loyalty* to those who have been feeling betrayed, *respect* to those who have been humiliated and de-dignified, *mirth* as appropriate and helpful for those who have been joyless, *creativity* to those who feel routinized in all they do and look for the joy of innovation. Every form of love is a personal expression of freedom. Love cannot exist without freedom.

Philosopher Thomas Jay Oord, who has been designated by various journals as one of the top five living theologians, has been our Institute's theologian of love and freedom since 2002. He coined the term "amipotence," "ami-" meaning "love" and "potence" meaning "power" as a substitute for omnipotent—or "all powerful"—the term often used to describe God's influence. Oord's major book on this topic is *The Death of Omnipotence and the Birth of Amipotence: Support and Criticism.*

Amipotence asserts that God would do anything to attract our awareness but will not violate our freedom. The One Mind is empowering but not overpowering. Love comes first and this is an absolute. This awesome love is within us too, but we must freely awaken to it. While the divine being may be authoritative, it is not authoritarian.

The amipotent God is what we can connect with, not an omnipotent one. The amipotent creator is what lies within our hearts and minds.

In the entire grand narrative of the Abrahamic faiths from the mythical Fall to the struggle for redemption, all is absurd without the idea of human freedom. Exodus would be a different story if the Jewish people had simply transferred their slavishness from Pharaoh to God. Slavish coercion was replaced by covenant freedom with all its wayward moments. A voluntary covenant replaced shackles. Jesus presumably could have resorted to coercion, and was tempted to do so in the desert, but he resisted. He renounced the external means of power. His truth nailed upon a cross forces no one; it must be accepted and confessed freely.

When people realize that freedom is their very deepest spiritual calling, because freedom is what they are, then they will follow their callings, listen to the still small voice within, and stay on the path. This freedom lies within the lofty human soul as given from the One Original Mind of which we are some small drop.

The Hindus have an expression, "Thou art That," which means that to know thyself is to become aware of *love, creativity, and freedom*—the essential godly qualities that lie within each of us. This love, however, is uncontrolling. It cannot violate the freedom of any human being and is therefore not omnipotent. It is amipotent, which ensures the power of attraction in the Supreme. We can respond to its qualities and the beauty of the created universe.

Concluding Thoughts

I am free because I love, and I can love because I am a free being. I am never free when I am entrapped in destructive emotions like resentment, bitterness, or hatred. I am never free when I do harm to others or even think about such a thing. I am free because early every day I meditate on Pure Unlimited Love and how it can take form in the encounters that lie before me. In this mindset and heartset, my soul flies light, and I manage the day with grace. The spirit of freedom projects into the world from our hearts and minds in awareness of the Supreme. In a simple formula,

$$\text{One Mind} + \text{One Heart} = \text{Inner Peace}$$

Epilogue

In 1959, novelist C. P. Snow described "a gulf of mutual incomprehension" between scientists and literary intellectuals, or humanists, regarding questions about nature, human nature, and the cosmos.[150] This gulf remains wide today, making deeper progress in our understanding of our relationship to the universe more difficult. Yet when progress on such questions occurs, it is usually synergistic.

Tremendous intellectual generativity exists in those areas where deep integration has occurred, such as in the study of empathy and altruism, mind and brain, neuroscience and ethics, science and religion, positive psychology, and bioethics. Still, there is a countervailing tendency, especially among academicians, toward the safe silos of sharp disciplinary boundaries. Scientists and humanists in a synergistic rapprochement, with exemplary integrative thinkers at the table, can do what neither can achieve alone.

I am not a scientific visionary who views human dignity in large part as a matter of seizing the opportunity to modify and enhance the species in fundamental ways through genetic engineering, the man/machine symbiosis of nanotechnology and cybernetics, robotics, reproductive cloning, and even the downloading of mind into immortalizing computers.

I am a prohumanist, asserting that our dignity lies chiefly in accepting the existing contours of human nature as the fine-tuned gift of evolutionary processes, and that biotechnological efforts beyond the therapeutic intended to re-create that nature are arrogant and shortsighted impositions on future generations. No technological modifications can provide genuine purpose, inner peace, wisdom, compassionate love, and similar virtues that make for a good life. A pure scientism with regard to human progress is unworthy of our dignity as human creatures. I endorse the natural human capacity for compassionate love, for it is the discovery of what already lies within us that dignifies what lies before us.

To get the best out of human nature, we must work with the best of what we have. And what is best in human nature? The most universal claim, readily articulated in all worthy spiritual and moral traditions over the centuries, is pure love.

We are bombarded by offers to enhance us as human beings. Botox, anabolic steroids, human growth hormone to make our children a little taller, and the dubious promises of a fountain of youth are all for sale, but none adds to dignity or a deeper inner peace. Let us instead focus our attention not on the external vessel of our bodies but on the capacity for a generous love that already lies within us waiting only to be more fully unveiled and engaged. Not just human love even, but the divine love that is within our minds and hearts. Without this love, we are poor even if we do not know it. With this love, we grow in dignity and happiness.

In the giving of self lies the discovery of a deeper and more peaceful self. Here lies the perennial truth that unites all the great religions. And here lies the inner core of human enhancement and dignity, which has nothing to do with biotechnological tinkering. Our dignity rests not in gadgets and biotechnological wizardry. I see these every day in the medical center, and while they can do good, they can also push aside the love that heals. Rather, our dignity as human beings is already ours to claim when we treat others with love and justice and when we manifest virtues as varied as perseverance, kindness, faith, courage, forgiveness, gratitude, commitment, humility, integrity, and hope. The expressions of the ways of love from celebration and attentive listening to creativity and helping to loyalty and respect are all at the very heart of human dignity. Loyal friendship, a concern for the needy, and the worry we have over a wayward child who is not necessarily our own are what make us creatures of dignity and grace.

The future of human dignity does not flow from "future shock" opportunities to modify and enhance human nature in fundamental ways. Dignity's true future is in expanding the modern idea of love from the narrow domain of the nearest and dearest to all humanity at some level. Let us reemphasize a love that does justice. But let us use every technique of science to better understand how to give and glow in kindness, heal with kindness, raise caring children, follow our callings, know the One Mind, cherish the gift of nature, and honor the spirit of freedom.

Currently, technology is far too autonomous and a threat to the beautiful inner contours of the loving, virtuous human being. Technology tries to mount the shoulders of the sailor who climbs as high on the mast as possible in order to rise high above the waters of nature but only to see the boat capsize under the weight, tipping the mast into the waves below. How can we presume that the brave new world will be a better world? It will only be better if it is a world of love and justice, and these are things that lie within our hearts and minds if we look carefully.

Acknowledgments

I never sought support for writing this book. I have worked on this theme since I was fifteen years old at St. Paul's School, at Reed, at the University of Chicago, at Michigan, Case Western, and at Stony Brook. It is my calling for sure. But along the way I encountered so many great mentors, some deceased, including Professor James M. Gustafson, the Reverend William Eddy then of Christ Church in Tarrytown, and Sir John Templeton, whose vision made the Institute for Research on Pure Unlimited Love a possibility. Sir John wrote a brief suggestive essay on "pure unlimited love" that I promised him I would develop someday. Promises made, promised kept. But the ideas and structure herein are my own.

I thank my deeply loyal mentors Dr. John M. "Jack" and his wife, Josephine Templeton; Dr. Joseph M. Foley; Drs. Robert Haynie and Susan Wentz of Case Western; and Drs. Jeffrey S. Trilling, Krisha Mehta, Phyllis Migdal, and Maria Basile of Stony Brook Medicine; and the Reverend Dr. Craig Malbon.

I thank my editors: the kind and humble Fiona Hallowell, Karen Chernyaev, and my book agent, Linda Konner.

I thank all the board members of the Institute for Research on [Pure]Unlimited Love, including Colleen Kelly, Matthew T. Lee,

Cathy M. Lewis, Joni Marra, Rev. Dr. Thomas Jay Oord, Kathy Pender, Dr. Jo-Ann Triner, EdD (who helped editorially early on with chapter 3), Judy Watson, and Dr. Wentz (who helped editorially with chapter 2). I also thank the Institute's many advisors and researchers.

I wish to thank all the great people, too many to mention, who work with our Center for Medical Humanities, Compassionate Care, and Bioethics at the Renaissance School of Medicine of Stony Brook University. Equally, I wish to thank all those with whom I worked for twenty years at Case/University Hospitals of Cleveland and the Cleveland Clinic.

I am especially grateful to all the people with dementia, or with what I prefer to call "deep forgetfulness," with whom I have been honored to learn and work for decades. It is in their presence that I learn most about the power of love to connect to all humanity, no matter how imperiled.

I am grateful for my wonderful son who has found his callings, his older sister, and my wife of forty-four years, Mitsuko Post, for understanding the mind and soul of a scholar and teacher like me.

About the Author

Stephen G. Post, PhD, is a public speaker, social philosopher, and scholar in health and social sciences, philosophy, and global spirituality, as well as an opinion leader, mentor, and educator. He currently serves as director of the Center for Medical Humanities, Compassionate Care, and Bioethics at the Stony Brook University Renaissance School of Medicine. In 2001, with philanthropist Sir John Templeton (d. 2008), Dr. Post cofounded the Institute for Research on Unlimited Love: Spirituality, Compassion, and Service, an organization devoted to achieving cultural transformation through a blend of the highest levels of scientific research, spiritual-philosophical reflection, and effective practice.

Described by Martin Seligman in *Flourish* as one of "the stars of positive psychology," Dr. Post has spent much of his career researching and writing about the interface of spirituality and science. He is the first author of *Why Good Things Happen to Good People: How to Live a Longer, Happier, Healthier Life by the Simple Act of Giving* (Random House Broadway, 2008), an influential book that became the initial cornerstone of social prescribing—a movement to connect people with social outlets in their community to improve health and well-being—in Canada, the United Kingdom, and the United States. He also wrote *Dignity for Deeply*

Forgetful People (Johns Hopkins University Press, 2022), a culmination of Dr. Post's lifelong look into the way we care for people with Alzheimer's and other forms of dementia. His writings are widely quoted across many traditions, most recently in Rabbi Shai Held's best-selling *Judaism Is About Love: Recovering the Heart of Jewish Life*, Prince Ghazi's *Love in the Holy Quran*, and in the work of the Indian Institute for Advanced Studies on *The Nature of Universal Consciousness*. He finds awesome beauty in the Book of Common Prayer.

Through his writing, work, and leadership at the Institute and several of the nation's most distinguished medical schools, Dr. Post has a decades' long relationship with the media. A natural and inspirational speaker and interviewee, Dr. Post is forever answering invitations to be a keynote speaker and to interview for print, audio, video, and television programs. Dr. Post has been quoted in more than five thousand newspapers and magazines and featured on numerous television shows, including *The Daily Show*. He's been interviewed by leading newspapers around the world, including *The New York Times*, *The Wall Street Journal*, *The Washington Post*, the *Los Angeles Times*, the *Japan Times*, and many more.

Dr. Post is the author of more than four hundred articles in leading peer-reviewed journals such as *Science*, *The American Journal of Psychiatry*, *The New England Journal of Medicine*, *Psychosomatic Medicine*, *Journal of the American Academy of Religion*, *The Journal of Religion*, *JAMA*, *Alzheimer's & Dementia*, *Hypatia: A Journal of Feminist Philosophy*, and *Nature*. He served as editor-in-chief of the five-volume *Encyclopedia of Bioethics* (Macmillan Reference, 3rd edition), the definitive reference work for the field of bioethics and medical humanities selected for the Dartmouth Medal by the American Library Association. His book *The Moral Challenge of Alzheimer's Disease* (Johns Hopkins

University Press, 1995/2000) was named a "medical classic of the 20th century" by the *British Medical Journal.*

Dr. Post holds a doctorate in world religions, comparative ethics, and psychology of religion from the University of Chicago. He taught at the University of Chicago Pritzker School of Medicine, Fordham-Marymount University, and the Case Western Reserve University School of Medicine. Since 2008, Dr. Post has held a professorial position in the medical school at Stony Brook University. He is an elected member of the Philadelphia College of Physicians for "outstanding contributions to medicine," the New York Academy of Medicine, and the Royal Society of Medicine. He is a Founding Fellow of the International Society for Science and Religion (ISSR). Based at Cambridge University, the ISSR is the world's preeminent society devoted to understanding the intersection of science and religion.

Dr. Post is the recipient of dozens of awards, most notably the 2019 National Alpha Omega Alpha Honor Medical Society Professionalism Award, the most prestigious award given to medical school educators, for codeveloping the Professional Identity Formation curriculum of the Renaissance School of Medicine of Stony Brook University. He received the national Pioneer Medal for "outstanding leadership in healthcare" from HealthCare Chaplaincy USA, the Certificate of Special Recognition from the US Congress for creating the research field of altruistic love, and the national Distinguished Service Award from the Alzheimer's & Associated Disorders Association (one of only three recipients) for contributions to caregiving and affected families.

About the Institute for Research on Unlimited Love

The Institute for Research on Unlimited Love was founded in 2001 by Dr. Post, with the formative and philanthropic guidance of Sir John Templeton, who personally selected Dr. Post as president after an extensive search. The Institute seeks to achieve cultural transformation through a blend of the highest levels of scientific research, spiritual-philosophical reflection, and effective practice. To do this, the Institute funds research on unselfish love, spiritual practices, compassion, positive psychology, and much more. The Seven Paths featured in this book are based in part on the research framework that guides the Institute.

Since its beginnings, the Institute has conducted research with some of the nation's most renowned scientists and thought leaders. Established in Cleveland's University Circle with a team of twelve consultants, all of whom are now renowned (including Greg Fricchione, MD, currently director of the Benson-Henry Institute for Mind Body Medicine at Mass General), the Institute has supported dozens of conferences and seventy major research projects at various universities. The Works of Love Conference sponsored in 2003 attracted eight hundred scientists, spiritual thinkers, and love practitioners from more than forty nations for a full week. In 2016 the Institute organized and sponsored the annual youth conference at the United Nations on this theme, filling the headquarters.

Since its beginnings, the Institute and these Seven Paths have contributed to more than four thousand articles in many of the world's leading journals. Thanks to Dr. Martin Seligman, the Institute is credited for helping to initiate the positive psychology movement around the practice of kindness.

The Institute effectively married science and spirituality and continues to hold this relationship to the highest standards. In 2020, the Dalai Lama (who contributed the book's foreword) wrote to Dr. Post stating his appreciation for the Institute's "convergence of science and spirituality to benefit humanity" as uniquely focused on the great theme of "consciousness and interconnectedness." The Institute is now supporting Victor Chan, coauthor of the Dalai Lama's last two books on compassion and forgiveness, who has been charged by His Holiness to write his definitive biography based on sixty years of close collaboration.

Notes

Introduction

1. William Butler Yeats, "The Second Coming," Poets.org, https://poets.org/poem/second-coming, accessed October 10, 2024.
2. Jeffrey S. Trilling, MD, conversation with author, November 2024.
3. Sam Parnia et al., "Guidelines and Standards for the Study of Death and Recalled Experiences of Death—A Multidisciplinary Consensus Statement and Proposed Future Directions," *Annals of the New York Academy of Sciences* 1511, no. 1 (2022): 1–17, https://doi.org/10.1111/nyas.14740.
4. 1 John 4:8, 4:16.
5. Matthew T. Lee et al., *The Heart of Religion: Spiritual Empowerment, Benevolence, and the Experience of God's Love* (Oxford University Press, 2013), 81.
6. Exodus 3:14; 1 John 4:16.
7. Proverbs 23:7.

Chapter 1

8. Sir John Templeton, conversation with author, January 1992.
9. Stephen G. Post, "An Ethics of Love for Persons with Alzheimer's Disease," *Alzheimer's Care Quarterly* 2, no. 2 (2001): 23–30.
10. "UnitedHealthcare/VolunteerMatch Do Good Live Well Study: Reviewing the benefits of volunteering." March 2010, https://cdn.volunteermatch.org. Seven years later, UnitedHealthcare published online the "Doing Good Is Good for You" study with VolunteerMatch, which, based on a survey of 2,705 adults, again confirmed that people who do good and help others gain a sense of personal enrichment, are happier, and more satisfied with life, https://unitedhealthcaregroup.com.

11. Stephen G. Post, "Rx It's Good to Be Good (G2BG) 2017 Commentary: Prescribing Volunteerism for Health, Happiness, Resilience, and Longevity," *American Journal of Health Promotion* 31, no. 2 (2017): 164–72 (with "Opening Commentary" by S. S. Johnson, 163–64), https://doi.org/10.1177/0890117117695113.
12. "World Happiness Report 2016," under chapter 1, page 2, first para., https://worldhappiness.report/ed/2016/.
13. Post, "Rx It's Good to Be Good," 164–72.
14. Stephen Post and Jill Neimark, *Why Good Things Happen to Good People* (Broadway Books, 2007), 10.
15. Post, "Rx It's Good to Be Good," 164–72.
16. Post, *Why Good Things*, 10–13.
17. Stephen G. Post, *Unlimited Love* (Templeton Press, 2001), 89.
18. Stephen G. Post, "Altruism and Health: It's Good to Be Good," *International Journal of Behavioral Medicine* 12, no. 2 (2005): 66–77.
19. Post, "Rx It's Good to Be Good," 164–72.
20. Maria E. Pagano et al., "Helping Other Alcoholics in Alcoholics Anonymous and Drinking Outcomes: Findings from Project MATCH," *Journal of Studies on Alcohol and Drugs* 65, no. 6 (2024): 766–73, https://doi.org/10.15288/jsa.2004.65.766. See also Marc Galanter MD & Stephen G. Post, Guest Co-editors, *Alcoholism Treatment Quarterly* 32, no. 2, 3 (2014), Special Issue, "Alcoholics Anonymous: New Directions in Research on Spirituality and Recovery." This volume includes important articles by luminaries on AA research such as George E. Vaillant, John Kelly, Tom McGovern, and many others. Further treatments of this theme can be found in S.G. Post, ed., *Altruism and Health: Perspectives from Empirical Research*, New York: Oxford University Press, 2007, and in S.G. Post, B.R. Johnson, M.L. Lee, M. E. Pagano, "Humility and 12-Step Recovery: A Prolegomenon for the Empirical Investigation of a Cardinal Virtue in Alcoholics Anonymous," *Alcohol Treatment Quarterly*, 34, no. 3 (2016), 262–73.
21. Paul Arnstein et al., "From Chronic Pain Patient to Peer: Benefits and Risks of Volunteering," *Pain Management Nurses* 3, no. 3 (Sept. 2002): 94–103, https://doi.org/10.1053/jpmn.2002.126069.
22. Jerome Groopman, *The Anatomy of Hope: How People Prevail in the Face of Illness* (Random House, 2004), 173.
23. Gwynn B. Sullivan and Martin J. Sullivan, "Promoting Wellness in Cardiac Rehabilitation: Exploring the Role of Altruism," *Journal of Cardiovascular Nursing* 11, no. 3 (1997): 43–52, https://doi.org/10.1097/00005082-199704000-00005.

24. Corporation for National & Community Service, *The Health Benefits of Volunteering: A Review of Recent Research,* 2007, 10, www.nationalservice.gov.
25. Corporation for National & Community Service, *Health Benefits,* 10.
26. B. Clouette and P. Deslandes, "The Hartford Retreat for the Insane: An Early Example of the Use of 'Moral Treatment' in America," *Connecticut Medicine: The Journal of the Connecticut State Medical Society* 61, no. 9 (1997): 521–27.
27. Hannah M. C. Schreier et al., "Effect of Volunteering on Risk Factors for Cardiovascular Disease in Adolescents: A Randomized Controlled Trial," *JAMA Pediatrics* 167, no. 4 (2013): 327–32, https://doi.org/10.1001/jamapediatrics.2013.1100.
28. Hannah E. Phillips et al., "Motivation to Impact: Medical Student Volunteerism in the COVID 19 Pandemic," *Medical Science Educator* 32, no. 5 (2022): 1149–57, https//:doi.org/10.1007/s40670-022-01639-1.
29. Byron R. Johnson et al., "Positive Criminology and Rethinking the Response to Adolescent Addiction: Evidence on the Role of Social Support, Religiosity, and Service to Others," *International Journal of Criminology and Sociology* 5 (September 2016): 75–85, https://doi.org/10.6000/1929-4409.2016.05.16; Stephen G. Post et al., "Humility and 12-Step Recovery: A Prolegomenon for the Empirical Investigation of a Cardinal Virtue in Alcoholics Anonymous," *Alcohol Treatment Quarterly* 34, no. 3 (2016): 262–73, https://doi.org/10.1080/07347324.2016.1182817.
30. Laura M. Padilla-Walker et al., "Does Helping Keep Teens Protected? Longitudinal Bidirectional Relations Between Prosocial Behavior and Problem Behavior," *Child Development* 86, no. 6 (2015): 1759–72, https://doi.org/10.1111/cdev.12411.
31. James Youniss and Peter Levine, *Engaging Young People in Civic Life* (Vanderbilt University Press, 2009), 86.
32. Ming-Ching Luoh and A. Regula Herzog, "Individual Consequences of Volunteer and Paid Work in Old Age: Health and Mortality," *Journal of Health and Social Behavior* 43, no. 4 (2002): 490–509.
33. Rodlescia S. Sneed and Sheldon Cohen, "A Prospective Study of Volunteerism and Hypertension Risk in Older Adults," *Psychology and Aging* 28, no. 2 (2013): 578–86, https://doi.org/10.1037/a0032718. This does not mean that we should sacrifice the kids' education to donate to famine relief. We do owe our children an opportunity.
34. William H. Herndon and Jesse William Weik, *Herndon's Lincoln: The True Story of a Great Life,* vol. 3 (Belford-Clarke, 1890), 439.
35. Maya Angelou, *Rainbow in the Cloud: The Wisdom and Spirit of Maya Angelou* (Random House, 2014), 39.

36. Maya Angelou, conversation with author at Wake Forest University, October 1998.
37. 1 Corinthians 13:4.
38. Robert Haynie, conversation with author, late 1980s.
39. Robert R. Provine, *Laughter: A Scientific Investigation* (Penguin, 2001).
40. John 18:38.
41. Christopher Peterson and Martin Seligman, eds., *Character Strengths and Virtues: A Handbook and Classification* (American Psychological Association/Oxford University Press, 2004), 462.
42. Marc Galanter et al., "Spirituality-Based Recovery from Drug Addiction in the Twelve-Step Fellowship of Narcotics Anonymous," *Journal of Addiction Medicine* 7, no. 3 (2013): 189–95, https://doi.org/10.1097/ADM.0b013e31828a0265; Elena Salmoirago-Blotcher et al., "Frequency of Private Spiritual Activity and Cardiovascular Risk in Post-Menopausal Women: The Women's Health Initiative," *Annals of Epidemiology* 23, no. 5 (2013): 239–45, https://doi.org/10.1016/j.annepidem.2013.03.002; Maria E. Pagano et al., "Assessing Youth Participation in AA-Related Helping: Validity of the Service to Others in Sobriety (SOS) Questionnaire in an Adolescent Sample," *The American Journal on Addictions* 22, no. 1 (2013): 60–66, https://doi.org/10.1111/j.1521-0391.2013.00322.x.
43. Peter C. Wyer et al., "Relationship-Centered Care: Antidote, Guidepost or Blind Alley? The Epistemology of 21st Century Health Care," *Journal of Evaluation in Clinical Practice* 20, no. 6 (2014): 881–89, https://doi.org/10.1111/jep.12224.
44. Redford Williams and Virginia Williams, *Anger Kills: Seventeen Strategies for Controlling the Hostility That Can Harm Your Health* (HarperPerennial, 1993).
45. Stephen G. Post et al., "Routine, Empathic, and Compassionate Patient Care: Definitions, Development, Obstacles, Education and Beneficiaries," *Journal of Evaluation in Clinical Practice* 20, no. 6 (2014): 872–80, https://doi.org/10.1111/jep.12243.
46. Oleg Zaslavsky et al., "Dispositional Optimism and Terminal Decline in Global Quality of Life," *Developmental Psychology* 51, no. 6 (2015): 856–63, https://doi.org/10.1037/dev0000018.
47. Francis W. Peabody, "The Care of the Patient," *JAMA* 88, no. 12 (1927): 877–82, https://doi:10.1001/jama.1927.02680380001001.
48. Abigail Zuger, "Dissatisfaction with Medical Practice," *New England Journal of Medicine* 350, no. 1 (2004): 69–75, https://doi.org/10.1056/NEJMsr031703.
49. Liselotte N. Dyrbye et al., "Association of Clinical Specialty with Symptoms of Burnout and Career Choice Regret Among U.S. Resident Physicians," *JAMA* 320, no. 11 (2018): 1114–30, https://doi.org/10.1001/jama.2018.12615.

50. Tait D. Shanafelt, "Enhancing Meaning in Work: A Prescription for Preventing Physician Burnout and Promoting Patient-Centered Care," *JAMA* 302, no. 12 (2009): 1338–40, https://doi.org/10.1001/jama.2009.1385.
51. Stephen G. Post and Michael E. McCullough, "Kindness," in *Character Strengths and Virtues: A Handbook and Classification*, ed. Christopher Peterson and Martin Seligman (American Psychological Association/Oxford University Press, 2004), 325–35.
52. Stephen G. Post et al., "Humility and 12-Step Recovery," 262–73.
53. It's well-documented that Lincoln had mastered the six books of Euclid's *Elements*, from which this axiom is drawn. See Glenn W. LaFantasie, "Lincoln, Euclid, and the Satisfaction of Success," *Journal of the Abraham Lincoln Association* 41, no. 1 (2020): 24–46, http://hdl.handle.net/2027/spo.2629860.0041.104.
54. Abraham Lincoln, "The Gettysburg Address," delivered November 19, 1863, Gettysburg, Pennsylvania.
55. Tenelle Porter et al., "Clarifying the Content of Intellectual Humility: A Systematic Review and Integrative Framework," *Journal of Personality Assessment* 104, no. 1 (2021): 1–13, https://doi.org/10.1080/00223891.2021.1975725.
56. Dennis Whitcomb et al., "Intellectual Humility: Owning Our Limitations," *Philosophy and Phenomenological Research* 94, no. 3 (2017): 509–39, https://doi.org/10.1111/phpr.12228.
57. Elizabeth J. Krumrei-Mancuso and Steven V. Rouse, "The Development and Validation of the Comprehensive Intellectual Humility Scale," *Journal of Personality Assessment* 98, no. 2 (2016): 209–21, https://doi.org/10.1080/00223891.2015.1068174.
58. Marshall B. Rosenberg, *Nonviolent Communication: A Language of Life*, 3rd ed. (PuddleDancer Press, 2015).

Chapter 3

59. Marc Chagall, *My Life* (Da Capo Press, 1994), 81–82.
60. Sidney Alexander, *Marc Chagall: A Biography* (Cassell, 1978), 33.
61. Ryan D. Duffy et al., "Work as a Calling: A Theoretical Model," *Journal of Counseling Psychology* 65, no. 4 (2018): 423–39, https://doi.org/10.1037/cou0000276.
62. P. A. Boyle et al., "Effect of Purpose in Life on the Relation Between Alzheimer Disease Pathologic Changes on Cognitive Function in Advanced Age," *Archives of General Psychiatry* 69, no. 5 (2012): 499–504, https://doi.org/10.1001/archgenpsychiatry.2011.1487.

63. U.S. Bureau of Labor Statistics, "The 'Great Resignation' in Perspective," *Monthly Labor Review*, July 2022, https://www.bls.gov/opub/mlr/2022/article/the-great-resignation-in-perspective.htm.
64. Jo-Ann Triner, email communication with author, July 2024.
65. Gerald Beals, "Thomas Editon 'Quotes,'" ThomasEdison.com, accessed March 13, 2025, https://www.thomasedison.com/quotes.html.
66. Beals, "Thomas Edison."
67. M. A. Rosanoff, "Edison in His Laboratory," *Harpers Magazine*, September 1932.
68. The commonly quoted version of an incident recounted in F. L. Dyer and T. C. Martin, *Edison: His Life and Inventions* (1910): "I have gotten a lot of results! I know several thousand things that won't work," in Susan Ratcliffe, ed., *Oxford Essential Quotations*, 4th ed. (Oxford University Press, 2016), accessed March 5, 2025, https://www.oxfordreference.com/display/10.1093/acref/9780191826719.001.0001/q-oro-ed4-00003960.

Chapter 4

69. J. Kiley Hamlin et al., "Social Evaluation by Preverbal Infants," *Nature* 450 (November 2007): 557–59, https://doi.org/10.1038/nature06288.
70. Hamlin, "Social Evaluation," 557–59.
71. Bryan Vossekuil et al., *The Final Report and Findings of the "Safe School Initiative": Implications for the Prevention of School Attacks in the United States* (U.S. Secret Service and U.S. Department of Education, May 2002), https://www.govinfo.gov/app/details/ERIC-ED466024.
72. P. Connolly et al., *Too Young to Notice? The Cultural and Political Awareness of 3–6 Year Olds in Northern Ireland* (Community Relations Council, 2002), https://pure.ulster.ac.uk/en/publications/too-young-to-notice-the-cultural-and-political-awareness-of-3-6-y-3.
73. Legend of unknown origin, commonly attributed to the Cherokee.
74. Doug Johnson, "What Love Is . . . from Perspective of a Child," *The Ironton Tribune*, February 20, 2022, https://www.irontontribune.com/2022/02/20/what-love-is-from-perspective-of-a-child/. Most of the quotes were collected by Sean Keener, who as much as any researcher delves into the child's experience of love.
75. Vincent J. Felitti et al., "Relationship of Childhood Abuse and Household Dysfunction to Many of the Leading Causes of Death in Adults: The Adverse Childhood Experiences (ACE) Study," *American Journal of Preventive Medicine* 14, no. 4 (1998): 245–58, https://doi.org/10.1016/S0749-3797(98)00017-8.

76. Jennifer A. Campbell et al., "Associations Between Adverse Childhood Experiences, High-Risk Behaviors, and Morbidity in Adulthood," *American Journal of Preventive Medicine* 50, no. 3 (2016): 344–52, https://doi.org/10.1016/j.amepre.2015.07.022.
77. Michele Dillon and Paul Wink, *In the Course of a Lifetime: Tracing Religious Belief, Practice, and Change* (University of California Press, 2007).
78. Pitirim A. Sorokin, *Altruistic Love: A Study of American Good Neighbors and Christian-Catholic Saints* (Beacon Press, 1950), 57.
79. *Beyond Rhetoric: A New American Agenda for Children and Families* (National Commission on Children, 1991), https://eric.ed.gov/?id=ED336201.
80. John Boswell, *The Kindness of Strangers: The Abandonment of Children in Western Europe from Late Antiquity to the Renaissance* (University of Chicago Press, 1998), 433.
81. Boswell, *Kindness of Strangers*, 253.
82. Mary D. Salter Ainsworth et al., *Patterns of Attachment: A Psychological Study of the Strange Situation* (Lawrence Erlbaum, 1978).
83. Genesis 1:28.
84. Stephen G Post, "The Moral Meaning of Relinquishing an Infant: Reflections on Adoption," *Thought* 67, no. 2 (1992): 207–20, https://doi.org/10.5840/thought199267227.
85. Thomas Lickona, *How to Raise Kind Kids: And Get Respect, Gratitude, and a Happier Family in the Bargain* (Penguin, 2018).
86. Pitirim A. Sorokin, *The Ways and Power of Love: Types, Factors, and Techniques of Moral Transformation*, with an Introduction by S. G. Post (Templeton Press, 2002), 194–95.
87. Lickona, *How to Raise*, 138.
88. Lickona, *How to Raise*, 139.
89. Friedrich Nietzsche, *On the Genealogy of Morality* (Cambridge University Press, 2006), 112.
90. Hal Edward Runkel, *Screamfree Parenting: The Revolutionary Approach to Raising Your Kids by Keeping Your Cool* (Harmony, 2007).
91. Thomas D. Parsons, "Virtual Reality in Pediatric Psychology," *Pediatrics* 140, no. 2 (2017): S86–S91, https://doi.org/10.1542/peds.2016-1758I.
92. Victoria Dunckley, *Reset Your Child's Brain* (New World Library, 2015).
93. Jonathan Haidt, *The Anxious Generation: How the Great Rewiring of Childhood Is Causing an Epidemic of Mental Illness* (Penguin Press, 2024).
94. Runkel, *Screamfree Parenting*.
95. "Making Caring Common Project," Harvard Graduate School of Education, accessed May 18, 2018, https://mcc.gse.harvard.edu/.

96. Katherine Weare, *Evidence for the Impact of Mindfulness on Children and Young People*, The Mindfulness in Schools Project, April 2012.
97. Rhonda Sciortino, *How the Power of Kindness Creates Success at Home, at Work and in the World* (Hatherleigh Press, 2018).
98. Sorokin, *Altruistic Love*, 213.

Chapter 5

99. Erwin Schrödinger, *What Is Life? With Mind and Matter and Autobiographical Sketches*, rep. ed. (Cambridge University Press, 2012), 129.
100. Schrödinger, *What Is Life?*, 129.
101. Larry Dossey, *One Mind: How Our Individual Mind Is Part of a Greater Consciousness and Why It Matters* (Hay House LLC, 2014).
102. Robert Kanigel, *The Man Who Knew Infinity: A Life of the Genius Ramanujan* (Atria Books, Simon & Schuster, 2016).
103. Mihaly Csikszentmihalyi, *Flow: The Psychology of Optimal Experience* (HarperCollins, 1990).
104. Robert Frost, "Mending Wall," in *The Poetry of Robert Frost: The Collected Poems, Complete and Unabridged*, ed. Edward Connery Lathem (Henry Holt and Co., 1979), 33.
105. 1 Corinthians 3:16.
106. Luke 17:21.
107. Matthew T. Lee et al., *The Heart of Religion: Spiritual Empowerment, Benevolence, and the Experience of God's Love* (Oxford University Press, 2013), 187.
108. Dean Radin, *Entangled Minds: Extrasensory Experiences in a Quantum Reality* (Simon & Schuster, Paraview Pocket Books, 2006).
109. W. H. Auden, "Introduction," in *The Protestant Mystics: An Anthology of Spiritual Experience from Martin Luther to T. S. Eliot*, ed. Anne Fremantle (Mentor Books, 1965).
110. Thomas Berry, *The Dream of the Earth* (Counterpoint Press, 1988), 131.
111. Berry, *Dream*, 131.
112. Bob Dylan, "Bob Dylan FULL 60 Minutes Ed Bradley 2004 Interview," interview by Ed Bradley, *60 Minutes*, CBS, December 5, 2004, video, 1:08, https://www.youtube.com/watch?v=hOas0d-fFK8.
113. Isaiah 35:1–2.
114. William Butler Yeats, "The Second Coming," Poets.org, https://poets.org/poem/second-coming, accessed July 2023.
115. Gilbert: The Magazine of the Society of G.K. Chesterton, https://www.chesterton.org/gilbert/, accessed April 26, 2025.

116. Alcoholics Anonymous World Services, Inc., *Alcoholics Anonymous Comes of Age: A Brief History of A.A.* (Alcoholics Anonymous World Services, Inc., 1957), 64.

Chapter 6

117. Hazrat Inayat Khan, as anthologized in *Sublime Love: Essay and Anthology*, by Stuart Rose (Indica Books, 2007), 215.
118. Sir John Templeton, *The Essential Worldwide Laws of Life* (Templeton Foundation, 2012), 133.
119. Ken Wilber, ed., *Quantum Questions: Mystical Writings of the World's Great Physicists* (Shambhala, 2001), 3.
120. Mahatma K. Ghandi, *The Law of Love* (Bharatiya Vidya Bhavan, 1970), 5. Emphasis added.
121. Ghandi, *The Law*, 9. Emphasis added.
122. www.screenagersmovie.com
123. Scott D. Sampson, *How to Raise a Wild Child: The Art and Science of Falling in Love with Nature* (Mariner Books, 2016).
124. David Elkind in *The Hurried Child: Growing Up Too Fast Too Soon, Third Edition* (Persius Publishing, 2001).
125. Maria Monroy and Dacher Keltner, "Awe as a Pathway to Mental and Physical Health," *Perspectives on Psychological Science* 18, no. 2 (2022): 309–20, https://doi.org:10.1177/17456916221094856.
126. Virginia E. Sturm et al., "Big Smile, Small Self: Awe Walks Promote Prosocial Positive Emotions in Older Adults," *Emotion* 22, no. 5 (2022): 1044–58, https://doi.org/10.1037/emo0000876.
127. Rudolf Otto, *The Idea of the Holy: An Inquiry into the Non-Rational Factor in the Idea of the Divine and Its Relation to the Rational*, trans. John W. Harvey (Oxford University Press, 1926), 5.
128. Lisa Baldissera, *Emily Carr: Life and Work*.
129. Auden, "Introduction."
130. Walter Rauschenbusch, "Prayer for This World," in *School Chapel Services and Prayers*, Pew ed., 52 (Church Publishing, 2007).
131. Kahlil Gibran, *Kahlil Gibran's Little Book of Life*, ed. Neil Douglas-Klotz (Hampton Roads Publishing, 2018).
132. John Philip Newell, *Sacred Earth Sacred Soul: Celtic Wisdom for Reawakening to What Our Souls Know and Healing the World* (HarperOne, 2021).
133. Walt Whitman, "Song of Myself, 31," Poets.org, accessed March 3, 2025, https://poets.org/poem/song-myself-31.

134. John Muir, "Yellowstone National Park," in *John Muir: A Reading Bibliography by Kimes* (University of the Pacific Scholarly Commons, 1986), 516, https://scholarlycommons.pacific.edu/jmb/245.
135. Muir, "Yellowstone," 516.
136. Attendee of Dementia Guide Dog Workshop, email to author, February 2017.

Chapter 7

137. Nikolai Berdyaev, *Slavery and Freedom* (Sophia Perennis, 2023), 92.
138. Schrödinger, *What Is Life?*, 129.
139. Schrödinger, *What Is Life?*, 129.
140. 1: Corinthians 7:23. (New King James Version).
141. Micah 6:8.
142. Jim LaRue, in discussion with author, January 2004.
143. Stephen G. Post, *Dignity for Deeply Forgetful People: How Caregivers Manage the Challenges of Alzheimer's Disease* (Johns Hopkins University Press, 2022), 191–210.
144. James Truslow Adams, *The Epic of America* (Little, Brown, and Company, 1931), xvi.
145. *Marbury v. Madison* 5 U.S. 137 (1803).
146. U.S. Constitution, amend. 1, §1.
147. Matthew 4:4.
148. Georg Wilhelm Friedrich Hegel, "Georg Wilhelm Friedrich Hegel (1770–1831)," in *Crowned Masterpieces of Literature That Have Advanced Civilization, Vol. VI*, ed. David J. Brewer et al. (Ferd. P. Kaiser, 1902), 2146.
149. Sam Parnia et al., "Guidelines and Standards for the Study of Death and Recalled Experiences of Death—A Multidisciplinary Consensus Statement and Proposed Future Directions," *Annals of the New York Academy of Sciences* 1511, no. 1 (2022): 1–17, https://doi.org/10.1111/nyas.14740.
150. C. P. Snow, *The Two Cultures and the Scientific Revolution* (Cambridge University Press, 1961), 4.